My Mark Twain

MARK TWAIN AND MR. HOWELLS AT LAKEWOOD, 1908

My Mark Twain

WILLIAM DEAN HOWELLS

with a new Introduction by
THOMAS WORTHAM,
University of California, Los Angeles

DOVER PUBLICATIONS, INC.
Mineola, New York

9943

Copyright

Introduction copyright © 1997 by Thomas Wortham.
All rights reserved under Pan American and International
Copyright Conventions.

Published in Canada by General Publishing Company, Ltd., 30
Lesmill Road, Don Mills, Toronto, Ontario.
Published in the United Kingdom by Constable and Company,
Ltd., 3 The Lanchesters, 162–164 Fulham Palace Road, London W6
9ER.

Bibliographical Note

This Dover edition, first published in 1997, is an unabridged republication of the work originally published by Harper & Brothers Publishers, New York, 1910, under the title *My Mark Twain: Reminiscences and Criticisms*. A new introduction by Thomas Wortham has been added to the present edition.

Library of Congress Cataloging-in-Publication Data

Howells, William Dean, 1837–1920.
    My Mark Twain / William Dean Howells.
        p.   cm.
    Originally published: New York : Harper & Brothers, 1910.
    ISBN 0-486-29640-7 (pbk.)
    1. Twain, Mark, 1835–1910. 2. Authors, American–19th century–Biography. I. Title.
PS1331.H6   1997
818'.409–dc21
[B]   96-39016
                                            CIP

Manufactured in the United States of America
Dover Publications, Inc., 31 East 2nd Street, Mineola, N.Y. 11501

INTRODUCTION TO THE DOVER EDITION

Only the day before Mark Twain's death on April 21, 1910, William Dean Howells pleaded with Frederick A. Duneka, a literary editor at Harper and Brothers, not to press him into doing what both men knew Howells eventually would have to do: "You know I would *like* to write about Clemens; and if I did, it would be something unique, for I should tell him as I have known him for forty years: the most truthful man I *ever* knew. But don't make me–don't *let* me–promise till I get my head out of this cloud in which I have been living with the anxieties of the last two months.–It wrings my heart to think of Clemens dying." Howells's great distress was not caused so much by his knowledge of the approaching death of his old literary friend and comrade; a more immediate threat to that center of being that gave his life sustenance and meaning was the illness of his wife, Elinor Mead Howells, that would end with her death several weeks later on the sixth of May. But both Howells and Duneka knew that it was a foregone conclusion that America's foremost man of letters would eulogize the country's greatest literary celebrity in the pages of *Harper's Monthly,* and within a week Howells announced to the

Harpers' editor that he had already completed the first installment of his Mark Twain "memories" and that "the material holds out even beyond my hope." By the first of May the second installment was done; three weeks later the work was finished. He then set sail for Europe with his daughter, hoping to find in travel an interval of forgetfulness before he had to return home and begin the hard task of adjustment to a life impoverished by his recent losses.

Howells was a prolific writer, a true professional who could produce copy on demand in sometimes difficult situations. But the speed and circumstances of the composition of his reminiscences of Mark Twain are remarkable even for him and no doubt account in large part for the book's curious charm. Unlike Howells's other autobiographical writings, there is revealed here little of that anguish or humiliation that memory frequently generated when he came to craft the events and emotions of the past into meaningful patterns. Instead, one experiences in these pages the recovery through recollection of the exuberance of lost youth and the prosperity of middle years, the shared life he enjoyed for some forty years with Mark Twain. Attention to this task during these days of anguish and bereavement provided an opportunity of escape, no doubt, but an escape that is art's greatest gift to mankind, lost as it is in the senselessness of time and circumstance. In a life remarkably rich in friendships and literary associations, there was no one who stood higher in Howells's estimation or closer to his fraternal heart than Mark Twain. From their very first meeting, when the author of *Innocents Abroad* had come to Howells's office in Boston to thank him for having spoken kindly in the *Atlantic Monthly* of his recently published book (an incident Howells refers to in *My Mark Twain*), the two men immensely enjoyed each other's company. Clara Clemens later recalled Howells's frequent visits to her father's house as a time of great fun: "He always brought sunshine and cheer into the house as no one else could. . . . His sense of humor and capacity to show it refreshed the hearts of all. To see him and Father enjoy a funny story or joke together was a complete show in itself. Both of them red in the face from laughing. . . ! I am sure no children laughed with more abandon than they did." And of course they shared great sorrows, too, and the sympathy of understanding that is sometimes all we have to make sense out of what Tennyson called "the riddle of the painful earth."

The foundation of their friendship went deep into the bedrock of their strikingly similar youths. Both were young men from the middle-western provinces who first came to terms with the world of ideas and literature in the village print shop, what Abe Lincoln called the "poor boy's college." Both had important river connections, Clemens through his years as a pilot on Mississippi steamboats; Howells, more vicariously, through his Dean uncles, famous riverboat captains. Both came East, challenged the literary establishment, and made their decided marks upon the literary marketplace. Both married eastern women from families of far higher social rank than their own, and through the next several decades shared in the glories and fears of raising children of similar ages and childhood interests. And, of course, there was the literary work they shared, sometimes as active collaborators but more often as trusted readers and honest listeners (Howells even more so than Mark Twain, as is revealed so splendidly in their literary correspondence published a generation ago). Finally, they shared similar visions, what Edwin Cady, Howells's most understanding biographer, happily phrased "the world in midwestern eyes," a perspective that was profoundly modern, agnostic, democratic, alienated, rootless, sad and unsparingly honest. Certainly among their contemporaries, no one understood better than Howells the art and character of Mark Twain, and the reviews from the previous forty years that he gathered to be reprinted with his reminiscences still provide important insights and useful critical perspectives for the modern reader. But none of them approach the power of understanding of the man and his art that is demonstrated in "Memories," the long first part of *My Mark Twain*.

What Howells most wanted to reveal to his readers was Mark Twain's "humanity and his convictions" as a writer and as a man living in the world of social relationships and obligations. It is a remarkably truthful depiction, even when Howells's own sense of literary decorum prevented him from fully sharing with his reader the extremes of Mark Twain's words and actions. Out of respect for the love he felt for his old friend and ally, he desired to be as honest in his portrait as he felt Mark Twain had been in his own character; still, he was faced with the ageless problem of all biographers and memorialists: how to report candidly the facts of the life but not destroy the ideal of the man? At times it will seem to some that Howells is too willing to excuse his friend's foibles and excesses, but this is the generosity of love and admiration that in the end may reveal more truly to others the subject that is being studied. He knew Duneka was right when the editor objected to Howells having recalled in the first installment an occasion when

Mark Twain had been drunk; one may say in print, Duneka warned, that a man "has been a thief, a defaulter, dishonest in every way, worthless, a murderer perhaps, and the public will accept that, but to say a man has been drunk is to say a thing from which the reader instinctively recoils." Howells willingly canceled the offending passage, realizing that his casual remark would very likely be picked up by headline writers for many of the nation's newspapers. Balance and proportion were for Howells the hallmarks of true vision, and he would not let incident interfere with the greater truth he had to tell. His greatest fear was that he had let too much of himself be seen in the portrait. He wrote to a young English admirer at the time: "As for the M. T. papers, I know they are honest, or 'should be honest,' but as I think them over, I am sensible of much raw haste in them, and perhaps a braggy note." But it is this dimension of the sketches that gives them their greatest veracity; it is finally his loving testimony that brings into focus the meaning and power he found in the man known to the world as Mark Twain.

The response of the public to "My Memories of Mark Twain," first published in *Harper's Monthly* during the summer months of 1910 and then immediately reprinted—together with the old reviews and critical articles—in the book *My Mark Twain: Reminiscences and Criticisms,* was all Howells could have desired. From England he wrote to Duneka in early September: "I get letters by every mail about the Mark Twain papers. I hope for the sake of Franklin Square as well as my own that the book will be acceptable. If it were to do again I could do it twice as well. But all life is a belated conception of imperfection." The misgivings Howells had about his work, feelings experienced by every artist who struggles to transform his ideal into some concrete representation, were not shared by the early reviewers or the book's many admirers in the years since. The writer in *The Nation* summed it up well when he observed: "The genial spirit of the immortal fun-maker himself has touched the hundred pages of reminiscence with characteristic gayety, and it is a vivid picture one gets, not simply of 'the Lincoln of our literature,' but of a rare friendship between two richly endowed natures."

THOMAS WORTHAM

Los Angeles, California
December, 1996

CONTENTS

ILLUSTRATIONS

PART FIRST

MEMORIES

Mark Twain

MY MARK TWAIN

I

IT was in the little office of James T. Fields, over the book-store of Ticknor & Fields, at 124 Tremont Street, Boston, that I first met my friend of now forty-four years, Samuel L. Clemens. Mr. Fields was then the editor of *The Atlantic Monthly,* and I was his proud and glad assistant, with a pretty free hand as to manuscripts, and an unmanacled command of the book - notices at the end of the magazine. I wrote nearly all of them myself, and in 1869 I had written rather a long notice of a book just winning its way to universal favor. In this review I had intimated my reservations concerning the *Innocents Abroad,* but I had the luck, if not the sense, to recognize that it was such fun as we had not had before. I forget just what I said in praise of it, and it does not matter; it is enough that I praised it enough to satisfy the author. He now signified as much, and he stamped his gratitude into my memory with a story wonderfully allegorizing the situation, which the mock modesty of print forbids my repeating here. Throughout my long acquaintance with him his graphic touch was always allowing itself a freedom which I cannot bring my fainter pencil to illustrate. He had the

Southwestern, the Lincolnian, the Elizabethan breadth of parlance, which I suppose one ought not to call coarse without calling one's self prudish; and I was often hiding away in discreet holes and corners the letters in which he had loosed his bold fancy to stoop on rank suggestion; I could not bear to burn them, and I could not, after the first reading, quite bear to look at them. I shall best give my feeling on this point by saying that in it he was Shakespearian, or if his ghost will not suffer me the word, then he was Baconian.

At the time of our first meeting, which must have been well toward the winter, Clemens (as I must call him instead of Mark Twain, which seemed always somehow to mask him from my personal sense) was wearing a sealskin coat, with the fur out, in the satisfaction of a caprice, or the love of strong effect which he was apt to indulge through life. I do not know what droll comment was in Fields's mind with respect to this garment, but probably he felt that here was an original who was not to be brought to any Bostonian book in the judgment of his vivid qualities. With his crest of dense red hair, and the wide sweep of his flaming mustache, Clemens was not discordantly clothed in that sealskin coat, which afterward, in spite of his own warmth in it, sent the cold chills through me when I once accompanied it down Broadway, and shared the immense publicity it won him. He had always a relish for personal effect, which expressed itself in the white suit of complete serge which he wore in his last years, and in the Oxford gown which he put on for every possible occasion, and said he would like to wear all the time. That was not vanity in him, but a keen feeling for costume which the severity of our modern tailoring forbids men, though it flatters women to every excess in it; yet he also enjoyed the shock, the offence,

4

the pang which it gave the sensibilities of others. Then there were times he played these pranks for pure fun, and for the pleasure of the witness. Once I remember seeing him come into his drawing-room at Hartford in a pair of white cowskin slippers, with the hair out, and do a crippled colored uncle to the joy of all beholders. Or, I must not say all, for I remember also the dismay of Mrs. Clemens, and her low, despairing cry of, " Oh, Youth!" That was her name for him among their friends, and it fitted him as no other would, though I fancied with her it was a shrinking from his baptismal Samuel, or the vernacular Sam of his earlier companionships. He was a youth to the end of his days, the heart of a boy with the head of a sage; the heart of a good boy, or a bad boy, but always a wilful boy, and wilfulest to show himself out at every time for just the boy he was.

II

THERE is a gap in my recollections of Clemens, which
I think is of a year or two, for the next thing I remember of him is meeting him at a lunch in Boston given
us by that genius of hospitality, the tragically destined
Ralph Keeler, author of one of the most unjustly forgotten books, *Vagabond Adventures,* a true bit of picaresque autobiography. Keeler never had any money, to
the general knowledge, and he never borrowed, and he
could not have had credit at the restaurant where he
invited us to feast at his expense. There was T. B.
Aldrich, there was J. T. Fields, much the oldest of
our company, who had just freed himself from the
trammels of the publishing business, and was feeling
his freedom in every word; there was Bret Harte, who
had lately come East in his princely progress from
California; and there was Clemens. Nothing remains
to me of the happy time but a sense of idle and aimless and joyful talk-play, beginning and ending nowhere, of eager laughter, of countless good stories from
Fields, of a heat - lightning shimmer of wit from Aldrich, of an occasional concentration of our joint mockeries upon our host, who took it gladly; and amid the
discourse, so little improving, but so full of good fellowship, Bret Harte's fleering dramatization of Clemens's mental attitude toward a symposium of Boston
illuminates. "Why, fellows," he spluttered, "this is
the dream of Mark's life," and I remember the glance

from under Clemens's feathery eyebrows which betrayed his enjoyment of the fun. We had beefsteak with mushrooms, which in recognition of their shape Aldrich hailed as shoe-pegs, and to crown the feast we had an omelette soufflé, which the waiter brought in as flat as a pancake, amid our shouts of congratulations to poor Keeler, who took them with appreciative submission. It was in every way what a Boston literary lunch ought not to have been in the popular ideal which Harte attributed to Clemens.

Our next meeting was at Hartford, or, rather, at Springfield, where Clemens greeted us on the way to Hartford. Aldrich was going on to be his guest, and I was going to be Charles Dudley Warner's, but Clemens had come part way to welcome us both. In the good fellowship of that cordial neighborhood we had two such days as the aging sun no longer shines on in his round. There was constant running in and out of friendly houses where the lively hosts and guests called one another by their Christian names or nicknames, and no such vain ceremony as knocking or ringing at doors. Clemens was then building the stately mansion in which he satisfied his love of magnificence as if it had been another sealskin coat, and he was at the crest of the prosperity which enabled him to humor every whim or extravagance. The house was the design of that most original artist, Edward Potter, who once, when hard pressed by incompetent curiosity for the name of his style in a certain church, proposed that it should be called the English violet order of architecture; and this house was so absolutely suited to the owner's humor that I suppose there never was another house like it; but its character must be for recognition farther along in these reminiscences. The vividest impression which Clemens gave us two ravenous young Boston authors was of the satisfying, the surfeiting nature of subscription publication. An army of agents was overrunning the country with the prospectuses of his books, and delivering them by the scores of thousands in completed sale. Of the *Innocents Abroad* he said, " It sells right along just like the Bible," and *Roughing It* was swiftly following, without perhaps ever quite overtaking it in popularity. But he lectured Aldrich and me on the folly of that mode of publication in the trade which we had thought it the highest success to achieve a chance in. " Anything but subscription publication is printing for private circulation," he maintained, and he so won upon our greed and hope that on the way back to Boston we planned the joint authorship of a volume adapted to subscription publication. We got a very good name for it, as we believed, in *Memorable Murders,* and we never got farther with it, but by the time we reached Boston we were rolling in wealth so deep that we could hardly walk home in the frugal fashion by which we still thought it best to spare car fare; carriage fare we did not dream of even in that opulence.

III

THE visits to Hartford which had begun with this affluence continued without actual increase of riches for me, but now I went alone, and in Warner's European and Egyptian absences I formed the habit of going to Clemens. By this time he was in his new house, where he used to give me a royal chamber on the ground floor, and come in at night after I had gone to bed to take off the burglar alarm so that the family should not be roused if anybody tried to get in at my window. This would be after we had sat up late, he smoking the last of his innumerable cigars, and soothing his tense nerves with a mild hot Scotch, while we both talked and talked and talked, of everything in the heavens and on the earth, and the waters under the earth. After two days of this talk I would come away hollow, realizing myself best in the image of one of those locust-shells which you find sticking to the bark of trees at the end of summer. Once, after some such bout of brains, we went down to New York together, and sat facing each other in the Pullman smoker without passing a syllable till we had occasion to say, " Well, we're there." Then, with our installation in a now vanished hotel (the old Brunswick, to be specific), the talk began again with the inspiration of the novel environment, and went on and on. We wished to be asleep, but we could not stop, and he lounged through the rooms in the long nightgown which he always wore in preference to the pajamas which he despised, and told the story of his life, the inexhaustible, the fairy, the Arabian Nights story, which I could never tire of even when it began to be told over again. Or at times he would reason high—

> " Of Providence, foreknowledge, will and fate,
> Fixed fate, free will, foreknowledge absolute,"

walking up and down, and halting now and then, with a fine toss and slant of his shaggy head, as some bold thought or splendid joke struck him.

He was in those days a constant attendant at the church of his great friend, the Rev. Joseph H. Twichell, and at least tacitly far from the entire negation he came to at last. I should say he had hardly yet examined the grounds of his passive acceptance of his wife's belief, for it was hers and not his, and he held it unscanned in the beautiful and tender loyalty to her which was the most moving quality of his most faithful soul. I make bold to speak of the love between them, because without it I could not make him known to others as he was known to me. It was a greater part of him than the love of most men for their wives, and she merited all the worship he could give her, all the devotion, all the implicit obedience, by her surpassing force and beauty of character. She was in a way the loveliest person I have ever seen, the gentlest, the kindest, without a touch of weakness; she united wonderful tact with wonderful truth; and Clemens not only accepted her rule implicitly, but he rejoiced, he gloried in it. I am not sure that he noticed all her goodness in the actions that made it a heavenly vision to others, he so had the habit of her goodness; but if there was any forlorn and helpless creature in the room Mrs.

Clemens was somehow promptly at his side or hers; she was always seeking occasion of kindness to those in her household or out of it; she loved to let her heart go beyond the reach of her hand, and imagined the whole hard and suffering world with compassion for its structural as well as incidental wrongs. I suppose she had her ladyhood limitations, her female fears of etiquette and convention, but she did not let them hamper the wild and splendid generosity with which Clemens rebelled against the social stupidities and cruelties. She had been a lifelong invalid when he met her, and he liked to tell the beautiful story of their courtship to each new friend whom he found capable of feeling its beauty or worthy of hearing it. Naturally, her father had hesitated to give her into the keeping of the young strange Westerner, who had risen up out of the unknown with his giant reputation of burlesque humorist, and demanded guaranties, demanded proofs. " He asked me," Clemens would say, " if I couldn't give him the names of people who knew me in California, and when it was time to hear from them I heard from him. ' Well, Mr. Clemens,' he said, ' nobody seems to have a very good word for you.' I hadn't referred him to people that I thought were going to whitewash me. I thought it was all up with me, but I was disappointed. ' So I guess I shall have to back you myself.' "

Whether this made him faithfuler to the trust put in him I cannot say, but probably not; it was always in him to be faithful to any trust, and in proportion as a trust of his own was betrayed he was ruthlessly and implacably resentful. But I wish now to speak of the happiness of that household in Hartford which responded so perfectly to the ideals of the mother when the three daughters, so lovely and so gifted, were yet little children. There had been a boy, and " Yes, *I* killed him," Clemens once said, with the unsparing self-blame in which he would wreak an unavailing regret. He meant that he had taken the child out imprudently, and the child had taken the cold which he died of, but it was by no means certain this was through its father's imprudence. I never heard him speak of his son except that once, but no doubt in his deep heart his loss was irreparably present. He was a very tender father and delighted in the minds of his children, but he was wise enough to leave their training altogether to the wisdom of their mother. He left them to that in everything, keeping for himself the pleasure of teaching them little scenes of drama, learning languages with them, and leading them in singing. They came to the table with their parents, and could have set him an example in behavior when, in moments of intense excitement, he used to leave his place and walk up and down the room, flying his napkin and talking and talking.

It was after his first English sojourn that I used to visit him, and he was then full of praise of everything English: the English personal independence and public spirit, and hospitality, and truth. He liked to tell stories in proof of their virtues, but he was not blind to the defects of their virtues: their submissive acceptance of caste, their callousness with strangers, their bluntness with one another. Mrs. Clemens had been in a way to suffer socially more than he, and she praised the English less. She had sat after dinner with ladies who snubbed and ignored one another, and left her to find her own amusement in the absence of the attention with which Americans perhaps cloy their guests, but which she could not help preferring. In their successive sojourns among them I believe he came to like the English less and she more; the fine delight of his first acceptance among them did not renew itself till his Oxford degree was given him; then it made his cup run over, and he was glad the whole world should see it.

His wife would not chill the ardor of his early Anglomania, and in this, as in everything, she wished to humor him to the utmost. No one could have realized more than she his essential fineness, his innate nobleness. Marriages are what the parties to them alone really know them to be, but from the outside I should say that this marriage was one of the most perfect. It lasted in his absolute devotion to the day of her death, that delayed long in cruel suffering, and that left one side of him in lasting night. From Florence there came to me heartbreaking letters from him about the torture she was undergoing, and at last a letter saying she was dead, with the simple-hearted cry, " I wish I was with Livy." I do not know why I have left saying till now that she was a very beautiful woman, classically regular in features, with black hair smooth over her forehead, and with tenderly peering, myopic eyes, always behind glasses, and a smile of angelic kindness. But this kindness went with a sense of humor which qualified her to appreciate the self-lawed genius of a man who will be remembered with the great humorists of all time, with Cervantes, with Swift, or with any others worthy his company; none of them was his equal in humanity.

IV

CLEMENS had appointed himself, with the architect's connivance, a luxurious study over the library in his new house, but as his children grew older this study, with its carved and cushioned arm-chairs, was given over to them for a school-room, and he took the room above his stable, which had been intended for his coachman. There we used to talk together, when we were not walking and talking together, until he discovered that he could make a more commodious use of the billiard-room at the top of his house, for the purposes of literature and friendship. It was pretty cold up there in the early spring and late fall weather with which I chiefly associate the place, but by lighting up all the gas-burners and kindling a reluctant fire on the hearth we could keep it well above freezing. Clemens could also push the balls about, and, without rivalry from me, who could no more play billiards than smoke, could win endless games of pool, while he carried points of argument against imaginable differers in opinion. Here he wrote many of his tales and sketches, and for anything I know some of his books. I particularly remember his reading me here his first rough sketch of *Captain Stormfield's Visit to Heaven,* with the real name of the captain, whom I knew already from his many stories about him.

We had a peculiar pleasure in looking off from the high windows on the pretty Hartford landscape, and down from them into the tops of the trees clothing the hillside by which his house stood. We agreed that there was a novel charm in trees seen from such a vantage, far surpassing that of the farther scenery. He had not been a country boy for nothing; rather he had been a country boy, or, still better, a village boy, for everything that Nature can offer the young of our species, and no aspect of her was lost on him. We were natives of the same vast Mississippi Valley; and Missouri was not so far from Ohio but that we were akin in our first knowledges of woods and fields as we were in our early parlance. I had outgrown the use of mine through my greater bookishness, but I gladly recognized the phrases which he employed for their lasting juiciness and the long-remembered savor they had on his mental palate.

I have elsewhere sufficiently spoken of his unsophisticated use of words, of the diction which forms the backbone of his manly style. If I mention my own greater bookishness, by which I mean his less quantitative reading, it is to give myself better occasion to note that he was always reading some vital book. It might be some out-of-the-way book, but it had the root of the human matter in it: a volume of great trials; one of the supreme autobiographies; a signal passage of history, a narrative of travel, a story of captivity, which gave him life at first-hand. As I remember, he did not care much for fiction, and in that sort he had certain distinct loathings; there were certain authors whose names he seemed not so much to pronounce as to spew out of his mouth. Goldsmith was one of these, but his prime abhorrence was my dear and honored prime favorite, Jane Austen. He once said to me, I suppose after he had been reading some of my unsparing praises of her—I am always prais-

ing her, " *You* seem to think that woman could write,"
and he forbore withering me with his scorn, apparently
because we had been friends so long, and he more
pitied than hated me for my bad taste. He seemed not
to have any preferences among novelists; or at least
I never heard him express any. He used to read the
modern novels I praised, in or out of print; but I do
not think he much liked reading fiction. As for plays,
he detested the theatre, and said he would as lief do a
sum as follow a plot on the stage. He could not, or did
not, give any reasons for his literary abhorrences, and
perhaps he really had none. But he could have said
very distinctly, if he had needed, why he liked the
books he did. I was away at the time of his great
Browning passion, and I know of it chiefly from hear-
say; but at the time Tolstoy was doing what could be
done to make me over Clemens wrote, " That man
seems to have been to you what Browning was to me."
I do not know that he had other favorites among the
poets, but he had favorite poems which he liked to read
to you, and he read, of course, splendidly. I have forgotten what piece of John Hay's it was that he liked
so much, but I remembered how he fiercely revelled
in the vengefulness of William Morris's *Sir Guy of the
Dolorous Blast,* and how he especially exulted in the
lines which tell of the supposed speaker's joy in slaying
the murderer of his brother:

> "I am threescore years and ten,
>   And my hair is nigh turned gray,
> But I am glad to think of the moment when
>   I took his life away."

Generally, I fancy his pleasure in poetry was not great,
and I do not believe he cared much for the convention-
ally accepted masterpieces of literature. He liked to

find out good things and great things for himself; sometimes he would discover these in a masterpiece new to him alone, and then, if you brought his ignorance home to him, he enjoyed it, and enjoyed it the more the more you rubbed it in.

Of all the literary men I have known he was the most unliterary in his make and manner. I do not know whether he had any acquaintance with Latin, but I believe not the least; German he knew pretty well, and Italian enough late in life to have fun with it; but he used English in all its alien derivations as if it were native to his own air, as if it had come up out of American, out of Missourian ground. His style was what we know, for good and for bad, but his manner, if I may difference the two, was as entirely his own as if no one had ever written before. I have noted before this how he was not enslaved to the consecutiveness in writing which the rest of us try to keep chained to. That is, he wrote as he thought, and as all men think, without sequence, without an eye to what went before or should come after. If something beyond or beside what he was saying occurred to him, he invited it into his page, and made it as much at home there as the nature of it would suffer him. Then, when he was through with the welcoming of this casual and unexpected guest, he would go back to the company he was entertaining, and keep on with what he had been talking about. He observed this manner in the construction of his sentences, and the arrangement of his chapters, and the ordering or disordering of his compilations. I helped him with a Library of Humor, which he once edited, and when I had done my work according to tradition, with authors, times, and topics carefully studied in due sequence, he tore it all apart, and " chucked " the pieces in wherever the fancy

17

for them took him at the moment. He was right: we were not making a text-book, but a book for the pleasure rather than the instruction of the reader, and he did not see why the principle on which he built his travels and reminiscences and tales and novels should not apply to it; and I do not now see, either, though at the time it confounded me. On minor points he was, beyond any author I have known, without favorite phrases or pet words. He utterly despised the avoidance of repetitions out of fear of tautology. If a word served his turn better than a substitute, he would use it as many times in a page as he chose.

V

At that time I had become editor of *The Atlantic Monthly,* and I had allegiances belonging to the conduct of what was and still remains the most scrupulously cultivated of our periodicals. When Clemens began to write for it he came willingly under its rules, for with all his wilfulness there never was a more biddable man in things you could show him a reason for. He never made the least of that trouble which so abounds for the hapless editor from narrower-minded contributors. If you wanted a thing changed, very good, he changed it; if you suggested that a word or a sentence or a paragraph had better be struck out, very good, he struck it out. His proof-sheets came back each a veritable "mush of concession," as Emerson says. Now and then he would try a little stronger language than *The Atlantic* had stomach for, and once when I sent him a proof I made him observe that I had left out the profanity. He wrote back: " Mrs. Clemens opened that proof, and lit into the room with danger in her eye. What profanity? You see, when I read the manuscript to her I skipped that." It was part of his joke to pretend a violence in that gentlest creature which the more amusingly realized the situation to their friends.

I was always very glad of him and proud of him as a contributor, but I must not claim the whole merit, or the first merit of having him write for us. It was the publisher, the late H. O. Houghton, who felt the incongruity of his absence from the leading periodical of the country, and was always urging me to get him to write. I will take the credit of being eager for him, but it is to the publisher's credit that he tried, so far as the modest traditions of *The Atlantic* would permit, to meet the expectations in pay which the colossal profits of Clemens's books might naturally have bred in him. Whether he was really able to do this he never knew from Clemens himself, but probably twenty dollars a page did not surfeit the author of books that " sold right along just like the Bible."

We had several short contributions from Clemens first, all of capital quality, and then we had the series of papers which went mainly to the making of his great book, *Life on the Mississippi.* Upon the whole I have the notion that Clemens thought this his greatest book, and he was supported in his opinion by that of the *portier* in his hotel at Vienna, and that of the German Emperor, who, as he told me with equal respect for the preference of each, united in thinking it his best; with such far-sundered social poles approaching in its favor, he apparently found himself without standing for opposition. At any rate, the papers won instant appreciation from his editor and publisher, and from the readers of their periodical, which they expected to prosper beyond precedent in its circulation. But those were days of simpler acceptance of the popular rights of newspapers than these are, when magazines strictly guard their vested interests against them. The New York *Times* and the St. Louis *Democrat* profited by the advance copies of the magazine sent them to reprint the papers month by month. Together they covered nearly the whole reading territory of the Union, and the terms of their daily publication enabled them to anticipate the magazine in its own restricted field. Its subscription list was not enlarged in the slightest measure, and *The Atlantic Monthly* languished on the news-stands as undesired as ever.

VI

It was among my later visits to Hartford that we began to talk up the notion of collaborating a play, but we did not arrive at any clear intention, and it was a telegram out of the clear sky that one day summoned me from Boston to help with a continuation of *Colonel Sellers*. I had been a witness of the high joy of Clemens in the prodigious triumph of the first *Colonel Sellers,* which had been dramatized from the novel of *The Gilded Age*. This was the joint work of Clemens and Charles Dudley Warner, and the story had been put upon the stage by some one in Utah, whom Clemens first brought to book in the courts for violation of his copyright, and then indemnified for such rights as his adaptation of the book had given him. The structure of the play as John T. Raymond gave it was substantially the work of this unknown dramatist. Clemens never pretended, to me at any rate, that he had the least hand in it; he frankly owned that he was incapable of dramatization; yet the vital part was his, for the characters in the play were his as the book embodied them, and the success which it won with the public was justly his. This he shared equally with the actor, following the company with an agent, who counted out the author's share of the gate money, and sent him a note of the amount every day by postal card. The postals used to come about dinner-time, and Clemens would read them aloud to us in wild triumph.

One hundred and fifty dollars—two hundred dollars—three hundred dollars were the gay figures which they bore, and which he flaunted in the air before he sat down at table, or rose from it to brandish, and then, flinging his napkin into his chair, walked up and down to exult in.

By-and-by the popularity of the play waned, and the time came when he sickened of the whole affair, and withdrew his agent, and took whatever gain from it the actor apportioned him. He was apt to have these sudden surceases, following upon the intensities of his earlier interest; though he seemed always to have the notion of making something more of *Colonel Sellers*. But when I arrived in Hartford in answer to his summons, I found him with no definite idea of what he wanted to do with him. I represented that we must have some sort of plan, and he agreed that we should both jot down a scenario overnight and compare our respective schemes the next morning. As the author of a large number of little plays which have been privately presented throughout the United States and in parts of the United Kingdom, without ever getting upon the public stage except for the noble ends of charity, and then promptly getting off it, I felt authorized to make him observe that his scheme was as nearly nothing as chaos could be. He agreed hilariously with me, and was willing to let it stand in proof of his entire dramatic inability. At the same time he liked my plot very much, which ultimated Sellers, according to Clemens's intention, as a man crazed by his own inventions and by his superstition that he was the rightful heir to an English earldom. The exuberant nature of Sellers and the vast range of his imagination served our purpose in other ways. Clemens made him a spiritualist, whose specialty in the occult was materialization; he became on impulse an ardent temperance reformer, and he headed a procession of temperance ladies after disinterestedly testing the deleterious effects of liquor upon himself until he could not walk straight; always he wore a marvellous fire-extinguisher strapped on his back, to give proof in any emergency of the effectiveness of his invention in that way.

We had a jubilant fortnight in working the particulars of these things out. It was not possible for Clemens to write like anybody else, but I could very easily write like Clemens, and we took the play scene and scene about, quite secure of coming out in temperamental agreement. The characters remained for the most part his, and I varied them only to make them more like his than, if possible, he could. Several years after, when I looked over a copy of the play, I could not always tell my work from his; I only knew that I had done certain scenes. We would work all day long at our several tasks, and then at night, before dinner, read them over to each other. No dramatists ever got greater joy out of their creations, and when I reflect that the public never had the chance of sharing our joy I pity the public from a full heart. I still believe that the play was immensely funny; I still believe that if it could once have got behind the footlights it would have continued to pack the house before them for an indefinite succession of nights. But this may be my fondness.

At any rate, it was not to be. Raymond had identified himself with Sellers in the play-going imagination, and whether consciously or unconsciously we constantly worked with Raymond in our minds. But before this time bitter displeasures had risen between Clemens and Raymond, and Clemens was determined that Raymond should never have the play. He first offered it to several other actors, who eagerly caught at it, only to give it back with the despairing renunciation, "That is a Raymond play." We tried managers with it, but their only question was whether they could get Raymond to do it. In the mean time Raymond had provided himself with a play for the winter—a very good play, by Demarest Lloyd; and he was in no hurry for ours. Perhaps he did not really care for it; perhaps he knew when he heard of it that it must come to him in the end. In the end it did, from my hand, for Clemens would not meet him. I found him in a mood of sweet reasonableness, perhaps the more softened by one of those lunches which our publisher, the hospitable James R. Osgood, was always bringing people together over in Boston. He said that he could not do the play that winter, but he was sure that he should like it, and he had no doubt he would do it the next winter. So I gave him the manuscript, in spite of Clemens's charges, for his suspicions and rancors were such that he would not have had me leave it for a moment in the actor's hands. But it seemed a conclusion that involved success and fortune for us. In due time, but I do not remember how long after, Raymond declared himself delighted with the piece; he entered into a satisfactory agreement for it, and at the beginning of the next season he started with it to Buffalo, where he was to give a first production. At Rochester he paused long enough to return it, with the explanation that a friend had noted to him the fact that Colonel Sellers in the play was a lunatic, and insanity was so serious a thing that it could not be represented on the stage without outraging the sensibilities of the audience; or words to that effect. We were too far off to allege Hamlet to the contrary, or King Lear, or to instance the delight which generations of readers throughout the world had taken in the mad freaks of Don Quixote.

Whatever were the real reasons of Raymond for rejecting the play, we had to be content with those he gave, and to set about getting it into other hands. In this effort we failed even more signally than before, if that were possible. At last a clever and charming elocutionist, who had long wished to get himself on the stage, heard of it and asked to see it. We would have shown it to any one by this time, and we very willingly showed it to him. He came to Hartford and did some scenes from it for us. I must say he did them very well, quite as well as Raymond could have done them, in whose manner he did them. But now, late toward spring, the question was where he could get an engagement with the play, and we ended by hiring a theatre in New York for a week of trial performances.

Clemens came on with me to Boston, where we were going to make some changes in the piece, and where we made them to our satisfaction, but not to the effect of that high rapture which we had in the first draft. He went back to Hartford, and then the cold fit came upon me, and " in visions of the night, in slumberings upon the bed," ghastly forms of failure appalled me, and when I rose in the morning I wrote him: " Here is a play which every manager has put out-of-doors and which every actor known to us has refused, and now we go and give it to an elocutioner. We are fools." Whether Clemens agreed with me or not in my conclusion, he agreed with me in my premises, and we promptly bought our play off the stage at a cost of seven hundred dollars, which we shared between us. But Clemens was never a man to give up. I relinquished gratis all right and title I had in the play,

THE OLD "ATLANTIC MONTHLY" OFFICE, 124 TREMONT STREET

and he paid its entire expenses for a week of one-night stands in the country. It never came to New York; and yet I think now that if it had come, it would have succeeded. So hard does the faith of the unsuccessful dramatist in his work die!

VII

THERE is an incident of this time so characteristic of both men that I will yield to the temptation of giving it here. After I had gone to Hartford in response to Clemens's telegram, Matthew Arnold arrived in Boston, and one of my family called on his, to explain why I was not at home to receive his introduction: I had gone to see Mark Twain. " Oh, but he doesn't like *that* sort of thing, does he?" "He likes Mr. Clemens very much," my representative answered, "and he thinks him one of the greatest men he ever knew." I was still Clemens's guest at Hartford when Arnold came there to lecture, and one night we went to meet him at a reception. While his hand laxly held mine in greeting, I saw his eyes fixed intensely on the other side of the room. "Who—who in the world is that?" I looked and said, "Oh, that is Mark Twain." I do not remember just how their instant encounter was contrived by Arnold's wish, but I have the impression that they were not parted for long during the evening, and the next night Arnold, as if still under the glamour of that potent presence, was at Clemens's house. I cannot say how they got on, or what they made of each other; if Clemens ever spoke of Arnold, I do not recall what he said, but Arnold had shown a sense of him from which the incredulous sniff of the polite world, now so universally exploded, had already perished. It might well have done so with his first dra-

28

matic vision of that prodigious head. Clemens was then hard upon fifty, and he had kept, as he did to the end, the slender figure of his youth, but the ashes of the burnt-out years were beginning to gray the fires of that splendid shock of red hair which he held to the height of a stature apparently greater than it was, and tilted from side to side in his undulating walk. He glimmered at you from the narrow slits of fine blue-greenish eyes, under branching brows, which with age grew more and more like a sort of plumage, and he was apt to smile into your face with a subtle but amiable perception, and yet with a sort of remote absence; you were all there for him, but he was not all there for you.

VIII

I shall not try to give chronological order to my recollections of him, but since I am just now with him in Hartford I will speak of him in association with the place. Once when I came on from Cambridge he followed me to my room to see that the water was not frozen in my bath, or something of the kind, for it was very cold weather, and then hospitably lingered. Not to lose time in banalities I began at once from the thread of thought in my mind. "I wonder why we hate the past so," and he responded from the depths of his own consciousness, "It's so damned humiliating," which is what any man would say of his past if he were honest; but honest men are few when it comes to themselves. Clemens was one of the few, and the first of them among all the people I have known. I have known, I suppose, men as truthful, but not so promptly, so absolutely, so positively, so almost aggressively truthful. He could lie, of course, and did to save others from grief or harm; he was not stupidly truthful; but his first impulse was to say out the thing and everything that was in him. To those who can understand it will not be contradictory of his sense of humiliation from the past, that he was not ashamed for anything he ever did to the point of wishing to hide it. He could be, and he was, bitterly sorry for his errors, which he had enough of in his life, but he was not ashamed in that mean way. What he had done he owned to, good, bad, or indifferent, and if it was bad he was rather amused than troubled as to the effect in your mind. He would not obtrude the fact upon you, but if it were in the way of personal history he would not dream of withholding it, far less of hiding it. He was the readiest of men to allow an error if he were found in it. In one of our walks about Hartford, when he was in the first fine flush of his agnosticism, he declared that Christianity had done nothing to improve morals and conditions, and that the world under the highest pagan civilization was as well off as it was under the highest Christian influences. I happened to be fresh from the reading of Charles Loring Brace's *Gesta Christi; or, History of Humane Progress,* and I could offer him abundant proofs that he was wrong. He did not like that evidently, but he instantly gave way, saying he had not known those things. Later he was more tolerant in his denials of Christianity, but just then he was feeling his freedom from it, and rejoicing in having broken what he felt to have been the shackles of belief worn so long. He greatly admired Robert Ingersoll, whom he called an angelic orator, and regarded as an evangel of a new gospel—the gospel of free thought. He took the warmest interest in the newspaper controversy raging at the time as to the existence of a hell; when the noes carried the day, I suppose that no enemy of perdition was more pleased. He still loved his old friend and pastor, Mr. Twichell, but he no longer went to hear him preach his sane and beautiful sermons, and was, I think, thereby the greater loser. Long before that I had asked him if he went regularly to church, and he groaned out: "Oh yes, I go. It 'most kills me, but I go," and I did not need his telling me to understand that he went because his wife wished it. He did tell me, after they both ceased

31

to go, that it had finally come to her saying, "Well, if you are to be lost, I want to be lost with you." He could accept that willingness for supreme sacrifice and exult in it because of the supreme truth as he saw it. After they had both ceased to be formal Christians, she was still grieved by his denial of immortality, so grieved that he resolved upon one of those heroic lies, which for love's sake he held above even the truth, and he went to her, saying that he had been thinking the whole matter over, and now he was convinced that the soul did live after death. It was too late. Her keen vision pierced through his ruse, as it did when he brought the doctor who had diagnosticated her case as organic disease of the heart, and, after making him go over the facts of it again with her, made him declare it merely functional.

To make an end of these records as to Clemens's beliefs, so far as I knew them, I should say that he never went back to anything like faith in the Christian theology, or in the notion of life after death, or in a conscious divinity. It is best to be honest in this matter; he would have hated anything else, and I do not believe that the truth in it can hurt any one. At one period he argued that there must have been a cause, a conscious source of things; that the universe could not have come by chance. I have heard also that in his last hours or moments he said, or his dearest ones hoped he had said, something about meeting again. But the expression, of which they could not be certain, was of the vaguest, and it was perhaps addressed to their tenderness out of his tenderness. All his expressions to me were of a courageous renunciation of any hope of living again, or elsewhere seeing those he had lost. He suffered terribly in their loss, and he was not fool enough to try ignoring his grief. He knew that for this there were but two medicines; that it would wear itself out with the years, and that meanwhile there was nothing for it but those respites in which the mourner forgets himself in slumber. I remember that in a black hour of my own when I was called down to see him, as he thought from sleep, he said with an infinite, an exquisite compassion, " Oh, did I wake you, did I *wake* you?" Nothing more, but the look, the voice, were everything; and while I live they cannot pass from my sense.

IX

HE was the most caressing of men in his pity, but he had the fine instinct, which would have pleased Lowell, of never putting his hands on you—fine, delicate hands, with taper fingers, and pink nails, like a girl's, and sensitively quivering in moments of emotion; he did not paw you with them to show his affection, as so many of us Americans are apt to do. Among the half-dozen, or half-hundred, personalities that each of us becomes, I should say that Clemens's central and final personality was something exquisite. His casual acquaintance might know him, perhaps, from his fierce intensity, his wild pleasure in shocking people with his ribaldries and profanities, or from the mere need of loosing his rebellious spirit in that way, as anything but exquisite, and yet that was what in the last analysis he was. They might come away loathing or hating him, but one could not know him well without realizing him the most serious, the most humane, the most conscientious of men. He was Southwestern, and born amid the oppression of a race that had no rights as against ours, but I never saw a man more regardful of negroes. He had a yellow butler when I first began to know him, because he said he could not bear to order a white man about, but the terms of his ordering George were those of the softest entreaty which command ever wore. He loved to rely upon George, who was such a broken reed in some things, though so stanch in others, and the fervent Republican in politics that Clemens then liked him to be. He could interpret Clemens's meaning to the public without conveying his mood, and could render his roughest answer smooth to the person denied his presence. His general instructions were that this presence was to be denied all but personal friends, but the soft heart of George was sometimes touched by importunity, and once he came up into the billiard-room saying that Mr. Smith wished to see Clemens. Upon inquiry, Mr. Smith developed no ties of friendship, and Clemens said, " You go and tell Mr. Smith that I wouldn't come down to see the Twelve Apostles." George turned from the threshold where he had kept himself, and framed a paraphrase of this message which apparently sent Mr. Smith away content with himself and all the rest of the world.

The part of him that was Western in his Southwestern origin Clemens kept to the end, but he was the most desouthernized Southerner I ever knew. No man more perfectly sensed and more entirely abhorred slavery, and no one has ever poured such scorn upon the second-hand, Walter-Scotticized, pseudo-chivalry of the Southern ideal. He held himself responsible for the wrong which the white race had done the black race in slavery, and he explained, in paying the way of a negro student through Yale, that he was doing it as his part of the reparation due from every white to every black man. He said he had never seen this student, nor ever wished to see him or know his name; it was quite enough that he was a negro. About that time a colored cadet was expelled from West Point for some point of conduct " unbecoming an officer and gentleman," and there was the usual shabby philosophy in a portion of the press to the effect that a negro could never feel the claim of honor. The man was fifteen parts white, but, " Oh yes," Clemens said, with bitter irony, " it was that one part black that undid him." It made him a " nigger " and incapable of being a gentleman. It was to blame for the whole thing. The fifteen parts white were guiltless.

Clemens was entirely satisfied with the result of the Civil War, and he was eager to have its facts and meanings brought out at once in history. He ridiculed the notion, held by many, that " it was not yet time " to philosophize the events of the great struggle; that we must " wait till its passions had cooled," and " the clouds of strife had cleared away." He maintained that the time would never come when we should see its motives and men and deeds more clearly, and that now, now, was the hour to ascertain them in lasting verity. Picturesquely and dramatically he portrayed the imbecility of deferring the inquiry at any point to the distance of future years when inevitably the facts would begin to put on fable.

He had powers of sarcasm and a relentless rancor in his contempt which those who knew him best appreciated most. The late Noah Brooks, who had been in California at the beginning of Clemens's career, and had witnessed the effect of his ridicule before he had learned to temper it, once said to me that he would rather have any one else in the world down on him than Mark Twain. But as Clemens grew older he grew more merciful, not to the wrong, but to the men who were in it. The wrong was often the source of his wildest drolling. He considered it in such hopelessness of ever doing it justice that his despair broke in laughter.

X

I GO back to that house in Hartford, where I was so often a happy guest, with tenderness for each of its endearing aspects. Over the chimney in the library which had been cured of smoking by so much art and science, Clemens had written in perennial brass the words of Emerson, " The ornament of a house is the friends who frequent it," and he gave his guests a welcome of the simplest and sweetest cordiality: but I must not go aside to them from my recollections of him, which will be of sufficient garrulity, if I give them as fully as I wish. The windows of the library looked northward from the hillside above which the house stood, and over the little valley with the stream in it, and they showed the leaves of the trees that almost brushed them as in a Claude Lorraine glass. To the eastward the dining-room opened amply, and to the south there was a wide hall, where the voices of friends made themselves heard as they entered without ceremony and answered his joyous hail. At the west was a little semi-circular conservatory of a pattern invented by Mrs. Harriet Beecher Stowe, and adopted in most of the houses of her kindly neighborhood. The plants were set in the ground, and the flowering vines climbed up the sides and overhung the roof above the silent spray of a fountain companied by callas and other water-loving lilies. There, while we breakfasted, Patrick came in from the barn and sprinkled the pretty bower, which poured out its responsive perfume in the delicate accents of its varied blossoms. Breakfast was Clemens's best meal, and he sat longer at his steak and coffee than at the courses of his dinner; luncheon was nothing to him, unless, as might happen, he made it his dinner, and reserved the later repast as the occasion of walking up and down the room, and discoursing at large on anything that came into his head. Like most good talkers, he liked other people to have their say; he did not talk them down; he stopped instantly at another's remark and gladly or politely heard him through; he even made believe to find suggestion or inspiration in what was said. His children came to the table, as I have told, and after dinner he was apt to join his fine tenor to their trebles in singing.

Fully half our meetings were at my house in Cambridge, where he made himself as much at home as in Hartford. He would come ostensibly to stay at the Parker House, in Boston, and take a room, where he would light the gas and leave it burning, after dressing, while he drove out to Cambridge and stayed two or three days with us. Once, I suppose it was after a lecture, he came in evening dress and passed twenty-four hours with us in that guise, wearing an overcoat to hide it when we went for a walk. Sometimes he wore the slippers which he preferred to shoes at home, and if it was muddy, as it was wont to be in Cambridge, he would put a pair of rubbers over them for our rambles. He liked the lawlessness and our delight in allowing it, and he rejoiced in the confession of his hostess, after we had once almost worn ourselves out in our pleasure with the intense talk, with the stories and the laughing, that his coming almost killed her, but it was worth it.

In those days he was troubled with sleeplessness, or,

rather, with reluctant sleepiness, and he had various specifics for promoting it. At first it had been champagne just before going to bed, and we provided that, but later he appeared from Boston with four bottles of lager-beer under his arms; lager-beer, he said now, was the only thing to make you go to sleep, and we provided that. Still later, on a visit I paid him at Hartford, I learned that hot Scotch was the only soporific worth considering, and Scotch whiskey duly found its place on our sideboard. One day, very long afterward, I asked him if he were still taking hot Scotch to make him sleep. He said he was not taking anything. For a while he had found going to bed on the bath-room floor a soporific; then one night he went to rest in his own bed at ten o'clock, and had gone promptly to sleep without anything. He had done the like with the like effect ever since. Of course, it amused him; there were few experiences of life, grave or gay, which did not amuse him, even when they wronged him.

He came on to Cambridge in April, 1875, to go with me to the centennial ceremonies at Concord in celebration of the battle of the Minute Men with the British troops a hundred years before. We both had special invitations, including passage from Boston; but I said, Why bother to go into Boston when we could just as well take the train for Concord at the Cambridge station? He equally decided that it would be absurd; so we breakfasted deliberately, and then walked to the station, reasoning of many things as usual. When the train stopped, we found it packed inside and out. People stood dense on the platforms of the cars; to our startled eyes they seemed to project from the windows, and unless memory betrays me they lay strewn upon the roofs like brakemen slain at the post of duty.

Whether this was really so or not, it is certain that
the train presented an impenetrable front even to our
imagination, and we left it to go its way without the
slightest effort to board. We remounted the fame-worn
steps of Porter's Station, and began exploring North
Cambridge for some means of transportation overland
to Concord, for we were that far on the road by which
the British went and came on the day of the battle.
The liverymen whom we appealed to received us, some
with compassion, some with derision, but in either
mood convinced us that we could not have hired a cat
to attempt our conveyance, much less a horse, or vehicle
of any description. It was a raw, windy day, very
unlike the exceptionally hot April day when the routed
redcoats, pursued by the Colonials, fled panting back to
Boston, with "their tongues hanging out like dogs,"
but we could not take due comfort in the vision of
their discomfiture; we could almost envy them, for they
had at least got to Concord. A swift procession of
coaches, carriages, and buggies, all going to Concord,
passed us, inert and helpless, on the sidewalk in the
peculiarly cold mud of North Cambridge. We began
to wonder if we might not stop one of them and bribe
it to take us, but we had not the courage to try, and
Clemens seized the opportunity to begin suffering with
an acute indigestion, which gave his humor a very dis-
mal cast. I felt keenly the shame of defeat, and the
guilt of responsibility for our failure, and when a gay
party of students came toward us on the top of a tally-
ho, luxuriously empty inside, we felt that our chance
had come, and our last chance. He said that if I
would stop them and tell them who I was they would
gladly, perhaps proudly, give us passage; I contended
that if with his far vaster renown he would approach
them, our success would be assured. While we stood,

lost in this " contest of civilities," the coach passed us, with gay notes blown from the horns of the students, and then Clemens started in pursuit, encouraged with shouts from the merry party who could not imagine who was trying to run them down, to a rivalry in speed. The unequal match could end only in one way, and I am glad I cannot recall what he said when he came back to me. Since then I have often wondered at the grief which would have wrung those blithe young hearts if they could have known that they might have had the company of Mark Twain to Concord that day and did not.

We hung about, unavailingly, in the bitter wind a while longer, and then slowly, very slowly, made our way home. We wished to pass as much time as possible, in order to give probability to the deceit we intended to practise, for we could not bear to own ourselves baffled in our boasted wisdom of taking the train at Porter's Station, and had agreed to say that we had been to Concord and got back. Even after coming home to my house, we felt that our statement would be wanting in verisimilitude without further delay, and we crept quietly into my library, and made up a roaring fire on the hearth, and thawed ourselves out in the heat of it before we regained our courage for the undertaking. With all these precautions we failed, for when our statement was imparted to the proposed victim she instantly pronounced it unreliable, and we were left with it on our hands intact. I think the humor of this situation was finally a greater pleasure to Clemens than an actual visit to Concord would have been; only a few weeks before his death he laughed our defeat over with one of my family in Bermuda, and exulted in our prompt detection.

XI

FROM our joint experience in failing I argue that Clemens's affection for me must have been great to enable him to condone in me the final defection which was apt to be the end of our enterprises. I have fancied that I presented to him a surface of such entire trustworthiness that he could not imagine the depths of unreliability beneath it; and that never realizing it, he always broke through with fresh surprise but unimpaired faith. He liked, beyond all things, to push an affair to the bitter end, and the end was never too bitter unless it brought grief or harm to another. Once in a telegraph office at a railway station he was treated with such insolent neglect by the young lady in charge, who was preoccupied in a flirtation with a " gentleman friend," that emulous of the public spirit which he admired in the English, he told her he should report her to her superiors, and (probably to her astonishment) he did so. He went back to Hartford, and in due time the poor girl came to me in terror and in tears; for I had abetted Clemens in his action, and had joined my name to his in his appeal to the authorities. She was threatened with dismissal unless she made full apology to him and brought back assurance of its acceptance. I felt able to give this, and, of course, he eagerly approved; I think he telegraphed his approval. Another time, some years afterward, we sat down together in places near the end of a car, and a brakeman

came in looking for his official note-book. Clemens
found that he had sat down upon it, and handed it to
him; the man scolded him very abusively, and came
back again and again, still scolding him for having no
more sense than to sit down on a note-book. The patience
of Clemens in bearing it was so angelic that I saw fit
to comment, " I suppose you will report this fellow."
" Yes," he answered, slowly and sadly. " That's what
I should have done once. But now I remember that he
gets twenty dollars a month."

Nothing could have been wiser, nothing tenderer,
and his humanity was not for humanity alone. He
abhorred the dull and savage joy of the sportsman in
a lucky shot, an unerring aim, and once when I met
him in the country he had just been sickened by the
success of a gunner in bringing down a blackbird, and
he described the poor, stricken, glossy thing, how it lay
throbbing its life out on the grass, with such pity as
he might have given a wounded child. I find this a fit
place to say that his mind and soul were with those
who do the hard work of the world, in fear of those
who give them a chance for their livelihoods and un-
derpay them all they can. He never went so far in
socialism as I have gone, if he went that way at all,
but he was fascinated with *Looking Backward* and had
Bellamy to visit him; and from the first he had a
luminous vision of organized labor as the only present help for working - men. He would show that
side with such clearness and such force that you
could not say anything in hopeful contradiction; he
saw with that relentless insight of his that in the
Unions was the working-man's only present hope of
standing up like a man against money and the power
of it. There was a time when I was afraid that his
eyes were a little holden from the truth; but in the

very last talk I heard from him I found that I was wrong, and that this great humorist was as great a humanist as ever. I wish that all the work-folk could know this, and could know him their friend in life as he was in literature; as he was in such a glorious gospel of equality as the *Connecticut Yankee in King Arthur's Court.*

JAMES T. FIELDS

XII

Whether I will or no I must let things come into my story thoughtwise, as he would have let them, for I cannot remember them in their order. One night, while we were giving a party, he suddenly stormed in with a friend of his and mine, Mr. Twichell, and immediately began to eat and drink of our supper, for they had come straight to our house from walking to Boston, or so great a part of the way as to be ahungered and athirst. I can see him now as he stood up in the midst of our friends, with his head thrown back, and in his hand a dish of those escalloped oysters without which no party in Cambridge was really a party, exulting in the tale of his adventure, which had abounded in the most original characters and amusing incidents at every mile of their progress. They had broken their journey with a night's rest, and they had helped themselves lavishly out by rail in the last half; but still it had been a mighty walk to do in two days. Clemens was a great walker in those years, and was always telling of his tramps with Mr. Twichell to Talcott's Tower, ten miles out of Hartford. As he walked of course he talked, and of course he smoked. Whenever he had been a few days with us, the whole house had to be aired, for he smoked all over it from breakfast to bedtime. He always went to bed with a cigar in his mouth, and sometimes, mindful of my fire insurance, I went up and took it away, still burning, after he had fallen asleep. I do not know how much a man may smoke and live, but apparently he smoked as much as a man could, for he smoked incessantly.

He did not care much to meet people, as I fancied, and we were greedy of him for ourselves; he was precious to us; and I would not have exposed him to the critical edge of that Cambridge acquaintance which might not have appreciated him at, say, his transatlantic value. In America his popularity was as instant as it was vast. But it must be acknowledged that for a much longer time here than in England polite learning hesitated his praise. In England rank, fashion, and culture rejoiced in him. Lord mayors, lord chief justices, and magnates of many kinds were his hosts; he was desired in country houses, and his bold genius captivated the favor of periodicals which spurned the rest of our nation. But in his own country it was different. In proportion as people thought themselves refined they questioned that quality which all recognize in him now, but which was then the inspired knowledge of the simple-hearted multitude. I went with him to see Longfellow, but I do not think Longfellow made much of him, and Lowell made less. He stopped as if with the long Semitic curve of Clemens's nose, which in the indulgence of his passion for finding every one more or less a Jew he pronounced unmistakably racial. It was two of my most fastidious Cambridge friends who accepted him with the English, the European entirety — namely, Charles Eliot Norton and Professor Francis J. Child. Norton was then newly back from a long sojourn abroad, and his judgments were delocalized. He met Clemens as if they had both been in England, and rejoiced in his bold freedom from environment, and in the rich variety and boundless reach of his talk. Child was of a per-

sonal liberty as great in its fastidious way as that of
Clemens himself, and though he knew him only at
second hand, he exulted in the most audacious instance
of his grotesquery, as I shall have to tell by-and-by,
almost solely. I cannot say just why Clemens seemed
not to hit the favor of our community of scribes and
scholars, as Bret Harte had done, when he came on
from California, and swept them before him, disrupt-
ing their dinners and delaying their lunches with im-
punity; but it is certain he did not, and I had better
say so.

I am surprised to find from the bibliographical authorities that it was so late as 1875 when he came with
the manuscript of *Tom Sawyer,* and asked me to read
it, as a friend and critic, and not as an editor. I have
an impression that this was at Mrs. Clemens's instance
in his own uncertainty about printing it. She trusted
me, I can say with a satisfaction few things now give
me, to be her husband's true and cordial adviser, and
I was so. I believe I never failed him in this part,
though in so many of our enterprises and projects I
was false as water through my temperamental love of
backing out of any undertaking. I believe this never
ceased to astonish him, and it has always astonished
me; it appears to me quite out of character; though
it is certain that an undertaking, when I have entered upon it, holds me rather than I it. But however this immaterial matter may be, I am glad
to remember that I thoroughly liked *Tom Sawyer,*
and said so with every possible amplification. Very
likely, I also made my suggestions for its improvement;
I could not have been a real critic without that; and I
have no doubt they were gratefully accepted and, I
hope, never acted upon. I went with him to the horse-
car station in Harvard Square, as my frequent wont

was, and put him aboard a car with his MS. in his hand, stayed and reassured, so far as I counted, concerning it. ˙ I do not know what his misgivings were; perhaps they were his wife's misgivings, for she wished him to be known not only for the wild and boundless humor that was in him, but for the beauty and tenderness and " natural piety "; and she would not have had him judged by a too close fidelity to the rude conditions of Tom Sawyer's life. This is the meaning that I read into the fact of his coming to me with those doubts.

XIII

Clemens had then and for many years the habit of writing to me about what he was doing, and still more of what he was experiencing. Nothing struck his imagination, in or out of the daily routine, but he wished to write me of it, and he wrote with the greatest fulness and a lavish dramatization, sometimes to the length of twenty or forty pages, so that I have now perhaps fifteen hundred pages of his letters. They will no doubt some day be published, but I am not even referring to them in these records, which I think had best come to the reader with an old man's falterings and uncertainties. With his frequent absences and my own abroad, and the intrusion of calamitous cares, the rich tide of his letters was more and more interrupted. At times it almost ceased, and then it would come again, a torrent. In the very last weeks of his life he burst forth, and, though too weak himself to write, he dictated his rage with me for recommending to him a certain author whose truthfulness he could not deny, but whom he hated for his truthfulness to sordid and ugly conditions. At heart Clemens was romantic, and he would have had the world of fiction stately and handsome and whatever the real world was not; but he was not romanticistic, and he was too helplessly an artist not to wish his own work to show life as he had seen it. I was preparing to rap him back for these letters when I read that he had got home to die; he would have liked the rapping back.

He liked coming to Boston, especially for those luncheons and dinners in which the fertile hospitality of our publisher, Osgood, abounded. He dwelt equidistant from Boston and New York, and he had special friends in New York, but he said he much preferred coming to Boston; of late years he never went there, and he had lost the habit of it long before he came home from Europe to live in New York. At these feasts, which were often of after - dinner - speaking measure, he could always be trusted for something of amazing delightfulness. Once, when Osgood could think of no other occasion for a dinner, he gave himself a birthday dinner, and asked his friends and authors. The beautiful and splendid trooper-like Waring was there, and I recall how in the long, rambling speech in which Clemens went round the table hitting every head at it, and especially visiting Osgood with thanks for his ingenious pretext for our entertainment, he congratulated Waring upon his engineering genius and his hypnotic control of municipal governments. He said that if there was a plan for draining a city at a cost of a million, by seeking the level of the water in the down-hill course of the sewers, Waring would come with a plan to drain that town up-hill at twice the cost and carry it through the Common Council without opposition. It is hard to say whether the time was gladder at these dinners, or at the small lunches at which Osgood and Aldrich and I foregathered with him and talked the afternoon away till well toward the winter twilight.

He was a great figure, and the principal figure, at one of the first of the now worn-out Authors' Readings, which was held in the Boston Museum to aid a Longfellow memorial. It was the late George Parsons Lathrop (everybody seems to be late in these sad days) who imagined the reading, but when it came to a price for seats I can always claim the glory of fixing it at five dollars. The price if not the occasion proved irresistible, and the museum was packed from the floor to the topmost gallery. Norton presided, and when it came Clemens's turn to read he introduced him with such exquisite praises as he best knew how to give, but before he closed he fell a prey to one of those lapses of tact which are the peculiar peril of people of the greatest tact. He was reminded of Darwin's delight in Mark Twain, and how when he came from his long day's exhausting study, and sank into bed at midnight, he took up a volume of Mark Twain, whose books he always kept on a table beside him, and whatever had been his tormenting problem, or excess of toil, he felt secure of a good night's rest from it. A sort of blank ensued which Clemens filled in the only possible way. He said he should always be glad that he had contributed to the repose of that great man, whom science owed so much, and then without waiting for the joy in every breast to burst forth, he began to read. It was curious to watch his triumph with the house. His carefully studied effects would reach the first rows in the orchestra first, and ripple in laughter back to the standees against the wall, and then with a fine resurgence come again to the rear orchestra seats, and so rise from gallery to gallery till it fell back, a cataract of applause from the topmost rows of seats. He was such a practised speaker that he knew all the stops of that simple instrument man, and there is no doubt that these results were accurately intended from his unerring knowledge. He was the most consummate public performer I ever saw, and it was an incomparable pleasure to hear him lecture; on the platform he was the great and finished actor which he probably would not have been on the stage. He was fond of private theatricals, and liked to play in them with his children and their friends, in dramatizations of such stories of his as *The Prince and the Pauper;* but I never saw him in any of these scenes. When he read his manuscript to you, it was with a thorough, however involuntary, recognition of its dramatic qualities; he held that an actor added fully half to the character the author created. With my own hurried and half-hearted reading of passages which I wished to try on him from unprinted chapters (say, out of *The Undiscovered Country* or *A Modern Instance*) he said frankly that my reading could spoil anything. He was realistic, but he was essentially histrionic, and he was rightly so. What we have strongly conceived we ought to make others strongly imagine, and we ought to use every genuine art to that end.

XIV

THERE came a time when the lecturing which had been the joy of his prime became his loathing, loathing unutterable, and when he renounced it with indescribable violence. Yet he was always hankering for those fleshpots whose savor lingered on his palate and filled his nostrils after his withdrawal from the platform. The Authors' Readings when they had won their brief popularity abounded in suggestion for him. Reading from one's book was not so bad as giving a lecture written for a lecture's purpose, and he was willing at last to compromise. He had a magnificent scheme for touring the country with Aldrich and Mr. G. W. Cable and myself, in a private car, with a cook of our own, and every facility for living on the fat of the land. We should read only four times a week, in an entertainment that should not last more than an hour and a half. He would be the impresario, and would guarantee us others at least seventy-five dollars a day, and pay every expense of the enterprise, which he provisionally called the Circus, himself. But Aldrich and I were now no longer in those earlier thirties when we so cheerfully imagined *Memorable Murders* for subscription publication; we both abhorred public appearances, and, at any rate, I was going to Europe for a year. So the plan fell through except as regarded Mr. Cable, who, in his way, was as fine a performer as Clemens, and could both read and sing the matter of his books. On a far less stupendous scale they two made the rounds of the great lecturing circuit together. But I believe a famous lecture-manager had charge of them and travelled with them.

He was a most sanguine man, a most amiable person, and such a believer in fortune that Clemens used to say of him, as he said of one of his early publishers, that you could rely upon fifty per cent. of everything he promised. I myself many years later became a follower of this hopeful prophet, and I can testify that in my case at least he was able to keep ninety-nine, and even a hundred, per cent. of his word. It was I who was much nearer failing of mine, for I promptly began to lose sleep from the nervous stress of my lecturing and from the gratifying but killing receptions afterward, and I was truly in that state from insomnia which Clemens recognized in the brief letter I got from him in the Western city, after half a dozen wakeful nights. He sardonically congratulated me on having gone into "the lecture field," and then he said: " I know where you are *now*. You are in hell."

It was this perdition which he re-entered when he undertook that round-the-world lecturing tour for the payment of the debts left to him by the bankruptcy of his firm in the publishing business. It was not purely perdition for him, or, rather, it was perdition for only one-half of him, the author-half; for the actor-half it was paradise. The author who takes up lecturing without the ability to give histrionic support to the literary reputation which he brings to the crude test of his reader's eyes and ears, invokes a peril and a misery unknown to the lecturer who has made his first public from the platform. Clemens was victorious on the platform from the beginning, and it would be folly to pretend that he did not exult in his triumphs there. But I suppose, with the wearing nerves of middle life, he hated more and more the personal swarming of interest upon him, and all the inevitable clatter of the thing. Yet he faced it, and he labored round our tiresome globe that he might pay the uttermost farthing of debts which he had not knowingly contracted, the debts of his partners who had meant well and done ill, not because they were evil, but because they were unwise, and as unfit for their work as he was. " Pay what thou owest." That is right, even when thou owest it by the error of others, and even when thou owest it to a bank, which had not lent it from love of thee, but in the hard line of business and thy need.

Clemens's behavior in this matter redounded to his glory among the nations of the whole earth, and especially in this nation, so wrapped in commerce and so little used to honor among its many thieves. He had behaved like Walter Scott, as millions rejoiced to know, who had not known how Walter Scott had behaved till they knew it was like Clemens. No doubt it will be put to his credit in the books of the Recording Angel, but what the Judge of all the Earth will say of it at the Last Day there is no telling. I should not be surprised if He accounted it of less merit than some other things that Clemens did and was: less than his abhorrence of the Spanish War, and the destruction of the South-African republics, and our deceit of the Filipinos, and his hate of slavery, and his payment of his portion of our race's debt to the race of the colored student whom he saw through college, and his support of a poor artist for three years in Paris, and his loan of opportunity to the youth who became the most brilliant of our actor-dramatists, and his eager pardon of the thoughtless girl who was near paying the penalty of her impertinence with the loss of her place, and his remembering that the insolent brakeman got so few dollars a month, and his sympathy for working-men standing up to money in their Unions, and even his pity for the wounded bird throbbing out its little life on the grass for the pleasure of the cruel fool who shot it. These and the thousand other charities and beneficences in which he abounded, openly or secretly, may avail him more than the discharge of his firm's liabilities with the Judge of all the Earth, who surely will do right, but whose measures and criterions no man knows, and I least of all men.

He made no great show of sympathy with people in their anxieties, but it never failed, and at a time when I lay sick for many weeks his letters were of comfort to those who feared I might not rise again. His hand was out in help for those who needed help, and in kindness for those who needed kindness. There remains in my mind the dreary sense of a long, long drive to the uttermost bounds of the South End at Boston, where he went to call upon some obscure person whose claim stretched in a lengthening chain from his early days in Missouri—a most inadequate person, in whose vacuity the gloom of the dull day deepened till it was almost too deep for tears. He bore the ordeal with grim heroism, and silently smoked away the sense of it, as we drove back to Cambridge, in his slippered feet, sombrely musing, sombrely swearing. But he knew he had done the right, the kind thing, and he was content. He came the whole way from Hartford to go with me to a friendless play of mine, which Alessandro Salvini was giving in a series of matinées to houses never enlarging themselves beyond the count of the brave two hundred who sat it through, and he stayed my fainting spirit with a cheer beyond flagons, joining me in my joke at the misery of it, and carrying the fun farther.

Before that he had come to witness the æsthetic suicide of Anna Dickinson, who had been a flaming light of the political platform in the war days, and had been left by them consuming in a hapless ambition for the theatre. The poor girl had had a play written especially for her, and as Anne Boleyn she ranted and exhorted through the five acts, drawing ever nearer the utter defeat of the anti-climax. We could hardly look at each other for pity, Clemens sitting there in the box he had taken, with his shaggy head out over the corner and his slippered feet curled under him: he either went to a place in his slippers or he carried them with him, and put them on as soon as he could put off his boots. When it was so that we could not longer follow her failure and live, he began to talk of the absolute close of her career which the thing was, and how probably she had no conception that it was the end. He philosophized the mercifulness of the fact, and of the ignorance of most of us, when mortally sick or fatally wounded. We think it is not the end, because we have never ended before, and we do not see how we can end. Some can push by the awful hour and live again, but for Anna Dickinson there could be, and was, no such palingenesis. Of course we got that solemn joy out of reading her fate aright which is the compensation of the wise spectator in witnessing the inexorable doom of others.

XV

WHEN Messrs. Houghton & Mifflin became owners of
The Atlantic Monthly, Mr. Houghton fancied having
some breakfasts and dinners, which should bring the
publisher and the editor face to face with the contributors, who were bidden from far and near. Of
course, the subtle fiend of advertising, who has now
grown so unblushing bold, lurked under the covers at
these banquets, and the junior partner and the young
editor had their joint and separate fine anguishes of
misgiving as to the taste and the principle of them;
but they were really very simple-hearted and honestly
meant hospitalities, and they prospered as they ought,
and gave great pleasure and no pain. I forget some
of the " emergent occasions," but I am sure of a birthday dinner most unexpectedly accepted by Whittier,
and a birthday luncheon to Mrs. Stowe, and I think a
birthday dinner to Longfellow; but the passing years
have left me in the dark as to the pretext of that supper
at which Clemens made his awful speech, and came so
near being the death of us all. At the breakfasts and
luncheons we had the pleasure of our lady contributors'
company, but that night there were only men, and because of our great strength we survived.

I suppose the year was about 1879, but here the
almanac is unimportant, and I can only say that it was
after Clemens had become a very valued contributor
of the magazine, where he found himself to his own

great explicit satisfaction. He had jubilantly accepted our invitation, and had promised a speech, which it appeared afterward he had prepared with unusual care and confidence. It was his custom always to think out his speeches, mentally wording them, and then memorizing them by a peculiar system of mnemonics which he had invented. On the dinner-table a certain succession of knife, spoon, salt-cellar, and butter-plate symbolized a train of ideas, and on the billiard-table a ball, a cue, and a piece of chalk served the same purpose. With a diagram of these printed on the brain he had full command of the phrases which his excogitation had attached to them, and which embodied the ideas in perfect form. He believed he had been particularly fortunate in his notion for the speech of that evening, and he had worked it out in joyous self-reliance. It was the notion of three tramps, three dead-beats, visiting a California mining-camp, and imposing themselves upon the innocent miners as respectively Ralph Waldo Emerson, Henry Wadsworth Longfellow, and Oliver Wendell Holmes. The humor of the conception must prosper or must fail according to the mood of the hearer, but Clemens felt sure of compelling this to sympathy, and he looked forward to an unparalleled triumph.

But there were two things that he had not taken into account. One was the species of religious veneration in which these men were held by those nearest them, a thing that I should not be able to realize to people remote from them in time and place. They were men of extraordinary dignity, of the thing called *presence,* for want of some clearer word, so that no one could well approach them in a personally light or trifling spirit. I do not suppose that anybody more truly valued them or more piously loved them than Clemens himself, but the intoxication of his fancy carried him beyond the bounds of that regard, and emboldened him to the other thing which he had not taken into account—namely, the immense hazard of working his fancy out before their faces, and expecting them to enter into the delight of it. If neither Emerson, nor Longfellow, nor Holmes had been there, the scheme might possibly have carried, but even this is doubtful, for those who so devoutly honored them would have overcome their horror with difficulty, and perhaps would not have overcome it at all.

The publisher, with a modesty very ungrateful to me, had abdicated his office of host, and I was the hapless president, fulfilling the abhorred function of calling people to their feet and making them speak. When I came to Clemens I introduced him with the cordial admiring I had for him as one of my greatest contributors and dearest friends. Here, I said, in sum, was a humorist who never left you hanging your head for having enjoyed his joke; and then the amazing mistake, the bewildering blunder, the cruel catastrophe was upon us. I believe that after the scope of the burlesque made itself clear, there was no one there, including the burlesquer himself, who was not smitten with a desolating dismay. There fell a silence, weighing many tons to the square inch, which deepened from moment to moment, and was broken only by the hysterical and blood-curdling laughter of a single guest, whose name shall not be handed down to infamy. Nobody knew whether to look at the speaker or down at his plate. I chose my plate as the least affliction, and so I do not know how Clemens looked, except when I stole a glance at him, and saw him standing solitary amid his appalled and appalling listeners, with his joke dead on his hands. From a first glance at the great three whom his jest had made its theme, I was aware of Longfellow sitting upright, and regarding the humorist with an air of pensive puzzle, of Holmes busily writing on his menu, with a well-feigned effect of preoccupation, and of Emerson, holding his elbows, and listening with a sort of Jovian oblivion of this nether world in that lapse of memory which saved him in those later years from so much bother. Clemens must have dragged his joke to the climax and left it there, but I cannot say this from any sense of the fact. Of what happened afterward at the table where the immense, the wholly innocent, the truly unimagined affront was offered, I have no longer the least remembrance. I next remember being in a room of the hotel, where Clemens was not to sleep, but to toss in despair, and Charles Dudley Warner's saying, in the gloom, "Well, Mark, *you're* a funny fellow." It was as well as anything else he could have said, but Clemens seemed unable to accept the tribute.

I stayed the night with him, and the next morning, after a haggard breakfast, we drove about and he made some purchases of bric-à-brac for his house in Hartford, with a soul as far away from bric-à-brac as ever the soul of man was. He went home by an early train, and he lost no time in writing back to the three divine personalities which he had so involuntarily seemed to flout. They all wrote back to him, making it as light for him as they could. I have heard that Emerson was a good deal mystified, and in his sublime forgetfulness asked, Who was this gentleman who appeared to think he had offered him some sort of annoyance? But I am not sure that this is accurate. What I am sure of is that Longfellow, a few days after, in my study, stopped before a photograph of Clemens and said, " Ah, he is a *wag!*" and nothing more. Holmes told me, with deep emotion, such as a brother humorist might well feel, that he had not lost an instant in replying to Clemens's letter, and assuring him that there had not been the least offence, and entreating him never to think of the matter again. " He said that he was a fool, but he was God's fool," Holmes quoted from the letter, with a true sense of the pathos and the humor of the self-abasement.

To me Clemens wrote a week later, " It doesn't get any better; it burns like fire." But now I understand that it was not shame that burnt, but rage for a blunder which he had so incredibly committed. That to have conceived of those men, the most dignified in our literature, our civilization, as impersonable by three hoboes, and then to have imagined that he could ask them personally to enjoy the monstrous travesty, was a break, he saw too late, for which there was no repair. Yet the time came, and not so very long afterward, when some mention was made of the incident as a mistake, and he said, with all his fierceness, " But I don't admit that it *was* a mistake," and it was not so in the minds of all witnesses at second hand. The morning after the dreadful dinner there came a glowing note from Professor Child, who had read the newspaper report of it, praising Clemens's burlesque as the richest piece of humor in the world, and betraying no sense of incongruity in its perpetration in the presence of its victims. I think it must always have ground in Clemens's soul, that he was the prey of circumstances, and that if he had some more favoring occasion he could retrieve his loss in it by giving the thing the right setting. Not more than two or three years ago, he came to try me as to trying it again at a meeting of newspaper men in Washington. I had to own my fears, while I alleged Child's note on the other hand, but in the end he did not try it with the newspaper men. I do not know whether he has ever printed it or not, but since the thing happened I have often wondered how much offence there really was in it. I am not sure but the horror of the spectators read more indignation into the subjects of the hapless drolling than they felt. But it must have been difficult for them to bear it with equanimity. To be sure, they were not themselves mocked; the joke was, of course, beside them; nevertheless, their personality was trifled with, and I could only end by reflecting that if I had been in their place I should not have liked it myself. Clemens would have liked it himself, for he had the heart for that sort of wild play, and he so loved a joke that even if it took the form of a liberty, and was yet a good joke, he would have loved it. But perhaps this burlesque was not a good joke.

XVI

Clemens was oftenest at my house in Cambridge, but he was also sometimes at my house in Belmont; when, after a year in Europe, we went to live in Boston, he was more rarely with us. We could never be long together without something out of the common happening, and one day something far out of the common happened, which fortunately refused the nature of absolute tragedy, while remaining rather the saddest sort of comedy. We were looking out of my library window on that view of the Charles which I was so proud of sharing with my all-but-next-door neighbor, Doctor Holmes, when another friend who was with us called out with curiously impersonal interest, "Oh, see that woman getting into the water!" This would have excited curiosity and alarmed anxiety far less lively than ours, and Clemens and I rushed downstairs and out through my basement and back gate. At the same time a coachman came out of a stable next door, and grappled by the shoulders a woman who was somewhat deliberately getting down the steps to the water over the face of the embankment. Before we could reach them he had pulled her up to the driveway, and stood holding her there while she crazily grieved at her rescue. As soon as he saw us he went back into his stable, and left us with the poor wild creature on our hands. She was not very young and not very pretty, and we could not have flattered ourselves with the notion of anything romantic in her suicidal mania, but we could take her on the broad human level, and on this we proposed to escort her up Beacon Street till we could give her into the keeping of one of those kindly policemen whom our neighborhood knew. Naturally there was no policeman known to us or unknown the whole way to the Public Garden. We had to circumvent our charge in her present design of drowning herself, and walk her past the streets crossing Beacon to the river. At these points it needed considerable reasoning to overcome her wish and some active manœuvring in both of us to enforce our arguments. Nobody else appeared to be interested, and though we did not court publicity in the performance of the duty so strangely laid upon us, still it was rather disappointing to be so entirely ignored.

There are some four or five crossings to the river between 302 Beacon Street and the Public Garden, and the suggestions at our command were pretty well exhausted by the time we reached it. Still the expected policeman was nowhere in sight; but a brilliant thought occurred to Clemens. He asked me where the nearest police station was, and when I told him, he started off at his highest speed, leaving me in sole charge of our hapless ward. All my powers of suasion were now taxed to the utmost, and I began attracting attention as a short, stout gentleman in early middle life endeavoring to distrain a respectable female of her personal liberty, when his accomplice had abandoned him to his wicked design. After a much longer time than I thought *I* should have taken to get a policeman from the station, Clemens reappeared in easy conversation with an officer who had probably realized that he was in the company of Mark Twain, and was in no hurry to end the interview. He took possession of our captive, and we saw her no more. I now wonder that with our joint instinct for failure we ever got rid of her; but I am sure we did, and few things in life have given me greater relief. When we got back to my house we found the friend we had left there quite unruffled and not much concerned to know the facts of our adventure. My impression is that he had been taking a nap on my lounge; he appeared refreshed and even gay; but if I am inexact in these details he is alive to refute me.

XVII

A LITTLE after this Clemens went abroad with his
family, and lived several years in Germany. His letters still came, but at longer intervals, and the thread
of our intimate relations was inevitably broken. He
would write me when something I had written pleased
him, or when something signal occurred to him, or
some political or social outrage stirred him to wrath,
and he wished to free his mind in pious profanity.
During this sojourn he came near dying of pneumonia
in Berlin, and he had slight relapses from it after coming home. In Berlin also he had the honor of dining
with the German Emperor at the table of a cousin
married to a high officer of the court. Clemens was a
man to enjoy such a distinction; he knew how to take
it as a delegated recognition from the German people;
but as coming from a rather cockahoop sovereign who
had as yet only his sovereignty to value himself upon,
he was not very proud of it. He expressed a quiet dis-
dain of the event as between the imperiality and himself, on whom it was supposed to confer such glory,
crowning his life with the topmost leaf of laurel. He
was in the same mood in his account of an English
dinner many years before, where there was a " little
Scotch lord " present, to whom the English tacitly referred Clemens's talk, and laughed when the lord laughed, and were grave when he failed to smile. Of all the
men I have known he was the farthest from a snob,

though he valued recognition, and liked the flattery of the fashionable fair when it came in his way. He would not go out of his way for it, but like most able and brilliant men he loved the minds of women, their wit, their agile cleverness, their sensitive perception, their humorous appreciation, the saucy things they would say, and their pretty, temerarious defiances. He had, of course, the keenest sense of what was truly dignified and truly undignified in people; but he was not really interested in what we call society affairs; they scarcely existed for him, though his books witness how he abhorred the dreadful fools who through some chance of birth or wealth hold themselves different from other men.

Commonly he did not keep things to himself, especially dislikes and condemnations. Upon most current events he had strong opinions, and he uttered them strongly. After a while he was silent in them, but if you tried him you found him in them still. He was tremendously worked up by a certain famous trial, as most of us were who lived in the time of it. He believed the accused guilty, but when we met some months after it was over, and I tempted him to speak his mind upon it, he would only say. The man had suffered enough; as if the man had expiated his wrong, and he was not going to do anything to renew his penalty. I found that very curious, very delicate. His continued blame could not come to the sufferer's knowledge, but he felt it his duty to forbear it.

He was apt to wear himself out in the vehemence of his resentments; or, he had so spent himself in uttering them that he had literally nothing more to say. You could offer Clemens offences that would anger other men and he did not mind; he would account for them from human nature; but if he thought you had in any way played him false you were anathema and maranatha forever. Yet not forever, perhaps, for by-and-by, after years, he would be silent. There were two men, half a generation apart in their succession, whom he thought equally atrocious in their treason to him, and of whom he used to talk terrifyingly, even after they were out of the world. He went farther than Heine, who said that he forgave his enemies, but not till they were dead. Clemens did not forgive his dead enemies; their death seemed to deepen their crimes, like a base evasion, or a cowardly attempt to escape; he pursued them to the grave; he would like to dig them up and take vengeance upon their clay. So he said, but no doubt he would not have hurt them if he had had them living before him. He was generous without stint; he trusted without measure, but where his generosity was abused, or his trust betrayed, he was a fire of vengeance, a consuming flame of suspicion that no sprinkling of cool patience from others could quench; it had to burn itself out. He was eagerly and lavishly hospitable, but if a man seemed willing to batten on him, or in any way to lie down upon him, Clemens despised him unutterably. In his frenzies of resentment or suspicion he would not, and doubtless could not, listen to reason. But if between the paroxysms he were confronted with the facts he would own them, no matter how much they told against him. At one period he fancied that a certain newspaper was hounding him with biting censure and poisonous paragraphs, and he was filling himself up with wrath to be duly discharged on the editor's head. Later, he wrote me with a humorous joy in his mistake that Warner had advised him to have the paper watched for these injuries. He had done so, and how many mentions of him did I reckon he had found in three months? Just

two, and they were rather indifferent than unfriendly.
So the paper was acquitted, and the editor's life was
spared. The wretch never knew how near he was to
losing it, with incredible preliminaries of obloquy, and
a subsequent devotion to lasting infamy.

MARK TWAIN'S HOME AT HARTFORD

XVIII

His memory for favors was as good as for injuries, and he liked to return your friendliness with as loud a band of music as could be bought or bribed for the occasion. All that you had to do was to signify that you wanted his help. When my father was consul at Toronto during Arthur's administration, he fancied that his place was in danger, and he appealed to me. In turn I appealed to Clemens, bethinking myself of his friendship with Grant and Grant's friendship with Arthur. I asked him to write to Grant in my father's behalf, but No, he answered me, I must come to Hartford, and we would go on to New York together and see Grant personally. This was before, and long before, Clemens became Grant's publisher and splendid benefactor, but the men liked each other as such men could not help doing. Clemens made the appointment, and we went to find Grant in his business office, that place where his business innocence was afterward so betrayed. He was very simple and very cordial, and I was instantly the more at home with him, because his voice was the soft, rounded, Ohio River accent to which my years were earliest used from my steamboating uncles, my earliest heroes. When I stated my business he merely said, Oh no; that must not be; he would write to Mr. Arthur; and he did so that day; and my father lived to lay down his office, when he tired of it, with no urgence from above.

It is not irrelevant to Clemens to say that Grant seemed to like finding himself in company with two literary men, one of whom at least he could make sure of, and unlike that silent man he was reputed, he talked constantly, and so far as he might he talked literature. At least he talked of John Phœnix, that delightfulest of the early Pacific Slope humorists, whom he had known under his real name of George H. Derby, when they were fellow-cadets at West Point. It was mighty pretty, as Pepys would say, to see the delicate deference Clemens paid our plain hero, and the manly respect with which he listened. While Grant talked, his luncheon was brought in from some unassuming restaurant near by, and he asked us to join him in the baked beans and coffee which were served us in a little room out of the office with about the same circumstance as at a railroad refreshment-counter. The baked beans and coffee were of about the railroad - refreshment quality; but eating them with Grant was like sitting down to baked beans and coffee with Julius Cæsar, or Alexander, or some other great Plutarchan captain.

One of the highest satisfactions of Clemens's often supremely satisfactory life was his relation to Grant. It was his proud joy to tell how he found Grant about to sign a contract for his book on certainly very good terms, and said to him that he would himself publish the book and give him a percentage three times as large. He said Grant seemed to doubt whether he could honorably withdraw from the negotiation at that point, but Clemens overbore his scruples, and it was his unparalleled privilege, his princely pleasure, to pay the author a far larger check for his work than had ever been paid to an author before. He valued even more than this splendid opportunity the sacred mo-

ments in which their business brought him into the
presence of the slowly dying, heroically living man
whom he was so befriending; and he told me in
words which surely lost none of their simple pathos
through his report how Grant described his suffering.

The prosperity of this venture was the beginning
of Clemens's adversity, for it led to excesses of enterprise which were forms of dissipation. The young
sculptor who had come back to him from Paris mod-
elled a small bust of Grant, which Clemens multiplied
in great numbers to his great loss, and the success of
Grant's book tempted him to launch on publishing seas
where his bark presently foundered. The first and
greatest of his disasters was the Life of Pope Leo
XIII., which he came to tell me of, when he had imagined it, in a sort of delirious exultation. He had
no words in which to paint the magnificence of the
project, or to forecast its colossal success. It would
have a currency bounded only by the number of Cath-
olics in Christendom. It would be translated into every
language which was anywhere written or printed; it
would be circulated literally in every country of the
globe, and Clemens's book agents would carry the prospectuses and then the bound copies of the work to the
ends of the whole earth. Not only would every Catholic
buy it, but every Catholic must, as he was a good Catholic, as he hoped to be saved. It was a magnificent
scheme, and it captivated me, as it had captivated
Clemens; it dazzled us both, and neither of us saw the
fatal defect in it. We did not consider how often Cath-
olics could not read, how often when they could, they
might not wish to read. The event proved that whether
they could read or not the immeasurable majority did
not wish to read the life of the Pope, though it was

written by a dignitary of the Church and issued to the world with every sanction from the Vatican. The failure was incredible to Clemens; his sanguine soul was utterly confounded, and soon a silence fell upon it where it had been so exuberantly jubilant.

XIX

THE occasions which brought us to New York together were not nearly so frequent as those which
united us in Boston, but there was a dinner given him
by a friend which remains memorable from the fatuity
of two men present, so different in everything but
their fatuity. One was the sweet old comedian
Billy Florence, who was urging the unsuccessful
dramatist across the table to write him a play about
Oliver Cromwell, and giving the reasons why he
thought himself peculiarly fitted to portray the character of Cromwell. The other was a modestly millioned
rich man who was then only beginning to amass the
moneys afterward heaped so high, and was still in the
condition to be flattered by the condescension of a yet
greater millionaire. His contribution to our gayety
was the verbatim report of a call he had made upon
William H. Vanderbilt, whom he had found just about
starting out of town, with his trunks actually in the
front hall, but who had stayed to receive the narrator.
He had, in fact, sat down on one of the trunks, and
talked with the easiest friendliness, and quite, we were
given to infer, like an ordinary human being. Clemens
often kept on with some thread of the talk when we
came away from a dinner, but now he was silent, as if
" high sorrowful and cloyed "; and it was not till well
afterward that I found he had noted the facts from the
bitterness with which he mocked the rich man, and the
pity he expressed for the actor.

He had begun before that to amass those evidences against mankind which eventuated with him in his theory of what he called "the damned human race." This was not an expression of piety, but of the kind contempt to which he was driven by our follies and iniquities as he had observed them in himself as well as in others. It was as mild a misanthropy, probably, as ever caressed the objects of its malediction. But I believe it was about the year 1900 that his sense of our perdition became insupportable and broke out in a mixed abhorrence and amusement which spared no occasion, so that I could quite understand why Mrs. Clemens should have found some compensation, when kept to her room by sickness, in the reflection that now she should not hear so much about "the damned human race." He told of that with the same wild joy that he told of overhearing her repetition of one of his most inclusive profanities, and her explanation that she meant him to hear it so that he might know how it sounded. The contrast of the lurid blasphemy with her heavenly whiteness should have been enough to cure any one less grounded than he in what must be owned was as fixed a habit as smoking with him. When I first knew him he rarely vented his fury in that sort, and I fancy he was under a promise to her which he kept sacred till the wear and tear of his nerves with advancing years disabled him. Then it would be like him to struggle with himself till he could struggle no longer and to ask his promise back, and it would be like her to give it back. His profanity was the heritage of his boyhood and young manhood in social conditions and under the duress of exigencies in which everybody swore about as impersonally as he smoked. It is best to recognize the fact of it, and I do so the more readily because I cannot suppose the Recording

Angel really minded it much more than that Guardian
Angel of his. It probably grieved them about equally,
but they could equally forgive it. Nothing came of his
pose regarding " the damned human race " except his
invention of the Human Race Luncheon Club. This
was confined to four persons who were never all got together, and it soon perished of their indifference.

In the earlier days that I have more specially in
mind one of the questions that we used to debate a good
deal was whether every human motive was not selfish.
We inquired as to every impulse, the noblest, the holi-
est in effect, and he found them in the last analysis
of selfish origin. Pretty nearly the whole time of a
certain railroad run from New York to Hartford was
taken up with the scrutiny of the self-sacrifice of a
mother for her child, of the abandon of the lover who
dies in saving his mistress from fire or flood, of the
hero's courage in the field and the martyr's at the stake.
Each he found springing from the unconscious love of
self and the dread of the greater pain which the self-
sacrificer would suffer in forbearing the sacrifice. If
we had any time left from this inquiry that day, he
must have devoted it to a high regret that Napoleon
did not carry out his purpose of invading England, for
then he would have destroyed the feudal aristocracy, or
" reformed the lords," as it might be called now. He
thought that would have been an incalculable blessing
to the English people and the world. Clemens was
always beautifully and unfalteringly a republican.
None of his occasional misgivings for America im-
plicated a return to monarchy. Yet he felt passion-
ately the splendor of the English monarchy, and there
was a time when he gloried in that figurative poetry
by which the king was phrased as " the Majesty of
England." He rolled the words deep-throatedly out,

and exulted in their beauty as if it were beyond any other glory of the world. He read, or read *at,* English history a great deal, and one of the by-products of his restless invention was a game of English Kings (like the game of Authors) for children. I do not know whether he ever perfected this, but I am quite sure it was not put upon the market. Very likely he brought it to a practicable stage, and then tired of it, as he was apt to do in the ultimation of his vehement undertakings.

XX

HE satisfied the impassioned demand of his nature for incessant activities of every kind by taking a personal as well as a pecuniary interest in the inventions of others. At one moment " the damned human race " was almost to be redeemed by a process of founding brass without air bubbles in it; if this could once be accomplished, as I understood, or misunderstood, brass could be used in art-printing to a degree hitherto impossible. I dare say I have got it wrong, but I am not mistaken as to Clemens's enthusiasm for the process, and his heavy losses in paying its way to ultimate failure. He was simultaneously absorbed in the perfection of a type-setting machine, which he was paying the inventor a salary to bring to a perfection so expensive that it was practically impracticable. We were both printers by trade, and I could take the same interest in this wonderful piece of mechanism that he could; and it was so truly wonderful that it did everything but walk and talk. Its ingenious creator was so bent upon realizing the highest ideal in it that he produced a machine of quite unimpeachable efficiency. But it was so costly, when finished, that it could not be made for less than twenty thousand dollars, if the parts were made by hand. This sum was prohibitive of its introduction, unless the requisite capital could be found for making the parts by machinery, and Clemens spent many months in vainly trying to get this money together. In the mean time simpler machines had been invented and the market filled, and his investment of three hundred thousand dollars in the beautiful miracle remained permanent but not profitable. I once went with him to witness its performance, and it did seem to me the last word in its way, but it had been spoken too exquisitely, too fastidiously. I never heard him devote the inventor to the infernal gods, as he was apt to do with the geniuses he lost money by, and so I think he did not regard him as a traitor.

In these things, and in his other schemes for the *subiti guadagni* of the speculator and the " sudden making of splendid names " for the benefactors of our species, Clemens satisfied the Colonel Sellers nature in himself (from which he drew the picture of that wild and lovable figure), and perhaps made as good use of his money as he could. He did not care much for money in itself, but he luxuriated in the lavish use of it, and he was as generous with it as ever a man was. He liked giving it, but he commonly wearied of giving it himself, and wherever he lived he established an almoner, whom he fully trusted to keep his left hand ignorant of what his right hand was doing. I believe he felt no finality in charity, but did it because in its provisional way it was the only thing a man could do. I never heard him go really into any sociological inquiry, and I have a feeling that that sort of thing baffled and dispirited him. No one can read *The Connecticut Yankee* and not be aware of the length and breadth of his sympathies with poverty, but apparently he had not thought out any scheme for righting the economic wrongs we abound in. I cannot remember our ever getting quite down to a discussion of the matter; we came very near it once in the day of the vast wave of emotion sent over the world by *Looking Back-*

ward, and again when we were all so troubled by the great coal strike in Pennsylvania; in considering that he seemed to be for the time doubtful of the justice of the working-man's cause. At all other times he seemed to know that whatever wrongs the working-man committed work was always in the right.

When Clemens returned to America with his family, after lecturing round the world, I again saw him in New York, where I so often saw him while he was shaping himself for that heroic enterprise. He would come to me, and talk sorrowfully over his financial ruin, and picture it to himself as the stuff of some unhappy dream, which, after long prosperity, had culminated the wrong way. It was very melancholy, very touching, but the sorrow to which he had come home from his long journey had not that forlorn bewilderment in it. He was looking wonderfully well, and when I wanted the name of his elixir, he said it was plasmon. He was apt, for a man who had put faith so decidedly away from him, to take it back and pin it to some superstition, usually of a hygienic sort. Once, when he was well on in years, he came to New York without glasses, and announced that he and all his family, so astigmatic and myopic and old-sighted, had, so to speak, burned their spectacles behind them upon the instruction of some sage who had found out that they were a delusion. The next time he came he wore spectacles freely, almost ostentatiously, and I heard from others that the whole Clemens family had been near losing their eyesight by the miracle worked in their behalf. Now, I was not surprised to learn that "the damned human race" was to be saved by plasmon, if anything, and that my first duty was to visit the plasmon agency with him, and procure enough plasmon to secure my family against the ills it was heir to for evermore. I did not immediately understand that plasmon was one of the investments which he had made from " the substance of things hoped for," and in the destiny of a disastrous disappointment. But after paying off the creditors of his late publishing firm, he had to do something with his money, and it was not his fault if he did not make a fortune out of plasmon.

XXI

For a time it was a question whether he should not go back with his family to their old home in Hartford. Perhaps the father's and mother's hearts drew them there all the more strongly because of the grief written ineffaceably over it, but for the younger ones it was no longer the measure of the world. It was easier for all to stay on indefinitely in New York, which is a sojourn without circumstance, and equally the home of exile and of indecision. The Clemenses took a pleasant, spacious house at Riverdale, on the Hudson, and there I began to see them again on something like the sweet old terms. They lived far more unpretentiously than they used, and I think with a notion of economy, which they had never very successfully practised. I recall that at the end of a certain year in Hartford, when they had been saving and paying cash for everything, Clemens wrote, reminding me of their avowed experiment, and asking me to guess how many bills they had at New Year's; he hastened to say that a horse-car would not have held them. At Riverdale they kept no carriage, and there was a snowy night when I drove up to their handsome old mansion in the station carryall, which was crusted with mud as from the going down of the Deluge after transporting Noah and his family from the Ark to whatever point they decided to settle at provisionally. But the good talk, the rich talk, the talk that could never suffer poverty of mind or soul, was there, and we jubilantly found ourselves again in our middle youth. It was the mighty moment when Clemens was building his engines of war for the destruction of Christian Science, which superstition nobody, and he least of all, expected to destroy. It would not be easy to say whether in his talk of it his disgust for the illiterate twaddle of Mrs. Eddy's book, or his admiration of her genius for organization was the greater. He believed that as a religious machine the Christian Science Church was as perfect as the Roman Church and destined to be more formidable in its control of the minds of men. He looked for its spread over the whole of Christendom, and throughout the winter he spent at Riverdale he was ready to meet all listeners more than half-way with his convictions of its powerful grasp of the average human desire to get something for nothing. The vacuous vulgarity of its texts was a perpetual joy to him, while he bowed with serious respect to the sagacity which built so securely upon the everlasting rock of human credulity and folly.

An interesting phase of his psychology in this business was not only his admiration for the masterly policy of the Christian Science hierarchy, but his willingness to allow the miracles of its healers to be tried on his friends and family, if they wished it. He had a tender heart for the whole generation of empirics, as well as the newer sorts of scientitians, but he seemed to base his faith in them largely upon the failure of the regulars rather than upon their own successes, which also he believed in. He was recurrently, but not insistently, desirous that you should try their strange magics when you were going to try the familiar medicines.

XXII

The order of my acquaintance, or call it intimacy, with Clemens was this: our first meeting in Boston, my visits to him in Hartford, his visits to me in Cambridge, in Belmont, and in Boston, our briefer and less frequent meetings in Paris and New York, all with repeated interruptions through my absences in Europe, and his sojourns in London, Berlin, Vienna, and Florence, and his flights to the many ends, and odds and ends, of the earth. I will not try to follow the events, if they were not rather the subjective experiences, of those different periods and points of time which I must not fail to make include his summer at York Harbor, and his divers residences in New York, on Tenth Street and on Fifth Avenue, at Riverdale, and at Stormfield, which his daughter has told me he loved best of all his houses and hoped to make his home for long years.

Not much remains to me of the week or so that we had together in Paris early in the summer of 1904. The first thing I got at my bankers was a cable message announcing that my father was stricken with paralysis, but urging my stay for further intelligence, and I went about, till the final summons came, with my head in a mist of care and dread. Clemens was very kind and brotherly through it all. He was living greatly to his mind in one of those arcaded little hotels in the Rue de Rivoli, and he was free from all household duties to range with me. We drove together to make calls of digestion at many houses where he had got indigestion through his reluctance from their hospitality, for he hated dining out. But, as he explained, his wife wanted him to make these visits, and he did it, as he did everything she wanted. At one place, some suburban villa, he could get no answer to his ring, and he "hove" his cards over the gate just as it opened, and he had the shame of explaining in his unexplanatory French to the man picking them up. He was excruciatingly helpless with his cabmen, but by very cordially smiling and casting himself on the drivers' mercy he always managed to get where he wanted. The family was on the verge of their many moves, and he was doing some small errands; he said that the others did the main things, and left him to do what the cat might.

It was with that return upon the buoyant billow of plasmon, renewed in look and limb, that Clemens's universally pervasive popularity began in his own country. He had hitherto been more intelligently accepted or more largely imagined in Europe, and I suppose it was my sense of this that inspired the stupidity of my saying to him when we came to consider "the state of polite learning" among us, "You mustn't expect people to keep it up here as they do in England." But it appeared that his countrymen were only wanting the chance, and they kept it up in honor of him past all precedent. One does not go into a catalogue of dinners, receptions, meetings, speeches, and the like, when there are more vital things to speak of. He loved these obvious joys, and he eagerly strove with the occasions they gave him for the brilliancy which seemed so exhaustless and was so exhausting. His friends saw that he was wearing himself out, and it was not because of Mrs. Clemens's health alone that they were glad to have

him take refuge at Riverdale. The family lived there
two happy, hopeless years, and then it was ordered that
they should change for his wife's sake to some less
exacting climate. Clemens was not eager to go to Florence, but his imagination was taken as it would have
been in the old-young days by the notion of packing
his furniture into flexible steel cages from his house
in Hartford and unpacking it from them untouched
at his villa in Fiesole. He got what pleasure any man
could out of that triumph of mind over matter, but the
shadow was creeping up his life. One sunny afternoon
we sat on the grass before the mansion, after his wife
had begun to get well enough for removal, and we
looked up toward a balcony where by-and-by that lovely
presence made itself visible, as if it had stooped there
from a cloud. A hand frailly waved a handkerchief;
Clemens ran over the lawn toward it, calling tenderly:
" What? What?" as if it might be an asking for him
instead of the greeting it really was for me. It was
the last time I saw her, if indeed I can be said to have
seen her then, and long afterward when I said how
beautiful we all thought her, how good, how wise, how
wonderfully perfect in every relation of life, he cried
out in a breaking voice: " Oh, why didn't you ever
tell her? She thought you didn't like her." What a
pang it was then not to have told her, but how could we
have told her? His unreason endeared him to me more
than all his wisdom.

To that Riverdale sojourn belong my impressions of
his most violent anti-Christian Science rages, which
began with the postponement of his book, and softened
into acceptance of the delay till he had well-nigh forgotten his wrath when it come out. There was also
one of those joint episodes of ours, which, strangely
enough, did not eventuate in entire failure, as most of

our joint episodes did. He wrote furiously to me of a wrong which had been done to one of the most helpless and one of the most helped of our literary brethren, asking me to join with him in recovering the money paid over by that brother's publisher to a false friend who had withheld it and would not give any account of it. Our hapless brother had appealed to Clemens, as he had to me, with the facts, but not asking our help, probably because he knew he need not ask; and Clemens enclosed to me a very taking-by-the-throat message which he proposed sending to the false friend. For once I had some sense, and answered that this would never do, for we had really no power in the matter, and I contrived a letter to the recreant so softly diplomatic that I shall always think of it with pride when my honesties no longer give me satisfaction, saying that this incident had come to our knowledge, and suggesting that we felt sure he would not finally wish to withhold the money. Nothing more, practically, than that, but that was enough; there came promptly back a letter of justification, covering a very substantial check, which we hilariously forwarded to our beneficiary. But the helpless man who was so used to being helped did not answer with the gladness I, at least, expected of him. He acknowledged the check as he would any ordinary payment, and then he made us observe that there was still a large sum due him out of the moneys withheld. At this point I proposed to Clemens that we should let the nonchalant victim collect the remnant himself. Clouds of sorrow had gathered about the bowed head of the delinquent since we began on him, and my fickle sympathies were turning his way from the victim who was really to blame for leaving his affairs so unguardedly to him in the first place. Clemens made some sort of grim assent, and we dropped the matter. He was more used to ingratitude from those he helped than I was, who found being lain down upon not so amusing as he found my revolt. He reckoned I was right, he said, and after that I think we never recurred to the incident. It was not ingratitude that he ever minded; it was treachery that really maddened him past forgiveness.

XXIII

DURING the summer he spent at York Harbor I was only forty minutes away at Kittery Point, and we saw each other often; but this was before the last time at Riverdale. He had a wide, low cottage in a pine grove overlooking York River, and we used to sit at a corner of the veranda farthest away from Mrs. Clemens's window, where we could read our manuscripts to each other, and tell our stories, and laugh our hearts out without disturbing her. At first she had been about the house, and there was one gentle afternoon when she made tea for us in the parlor, but that was the last time I spoke with her. After that it was really a question of how soonest and easiest she could be got back to Riverdale; but, of course, there were specious delays in which she seemed no worse and seemed a little better, and Clemens could work at a novel he had begun. He had taken a room in the house of a friend and neighbor, a fisherman and boatman; there was a table where he could write, and a bed where he could lie down and read; and there, unless my memory has played me one of those constructive tricks that people's memories indulge in, he read me the first chapters of an admirable story. The scene was laid in a Missouri town, and the characters such as he had known in boyhood; but often as I tried to make him own it, he denied having written any such story; it is possible that I dreamed it, but I hope the MS. will yet be found.

XXIV

I CANNOT say whether or not he believed that his wife
would recover; he fought the fear of her death to the
end; for her life was far more largely his than the
lives of most men's wives are theirs. For his own life
I believe he would never have much cared, if I may
trust a saying of one who was so absolutely without
pose as he was. He said that he never saw a dead man
whom he did not envy for having had it over and being
done with it. Life had always amused him, and in the
resurgence of its interests after his sorrow had ebbed
away he was again deeply interested in the world and
in the human race, which, though damned, abounded
in subjects of curious inquiry. When the time came
for his wife's removal from York Harbor I went with
him to Boston, where he wished to look up the best
means of her conveyance to New York. The inquiry
absorbed him: the sort of invalid-car he could get;
how she could be carried to the village station; how
the car could be detached from the eastern train at
Boston and carried round to the southern train on the
other side of the city, and then how it could be attached
to the Hudson River train at New York and left at
Riverdale. There was no particular of the business
which he did not scrutinize and master, not only with
his poignant concern for her welfare, but with his
strong curiosity as to how these unusual things were
done with the usual means. With the inertness that

grows upon an aging man he had been used to delegating more and more things, but of that thing I perceived that he would not delegate the least detail.

He had meant never to go abroad again, but when it came time to go he did not look forward to returning; he expected to live in Florence always after that; they were used to the life and they had been happy there some years earlier before he went with his wife for the cure of Nauheim. But when he came home again it was for good and all. It was natural that he should wish to live in New York, where they had already had a pleasant year in Tenth Street. I used to see him there in an upper room, looking south over a quiet open space of back yards where we fought our battles in behalf of the Filipinos and the Boers, and he carried on his campaign against the missionaries in China. He had not yet formed his habit of lying for whole days in bed and reading and writing there, yet he was a good deal in bed, from weakness, I suppose, and for the mere comfort of it.

My perspectives are not very clear, and in the fore-shortening of events which always takes place in our review of the past I may not always time things aright. But I believe it was not until he had taken his house at 21 Fifth Avenue that he began to talk to me of writing his autobiography. He meant that it should be a perfectly veracious record of his life and period; for the first time in literature there should be a true history of a man and a true presentation of the men the man had known. As we talked it over the scheme enlarged itself in our riotous fancy. We said it should be not only a book, it should be a library, not only a library, but a literature. It should make good the world's loss through Omar's barbarity at Alexandria; there was no image so grotesque, so extravagant that

we did not play with it; and the work so far as he
carried it was really done on a colossal scale. But one
day he said that as to veracity it was a failure; he had
begun to lie, and that if no man ever yet told the truth
about himself it was because no man ever could. How
far he had carried his autobiography I cannot say; he
dictated the matter several hours each day; and the
public has already seen long passages from it, and can
judge, probably, of the make and matter of the whole
from these. It is immensely inclusive, and it observes
no order or sequence. Whether now, after his death, it
will be published soon or late I have no means of knowing. Once or twice he said in a vague way that it was
not to be published for twenty years, so that the dis-
comfort of publicity might be minimized for all the
survivors. Suddenly he told me he was not working at
it; but I did not understand whether he had finished
it or merely dropped it; I never asked.

We lived in the same city, but for old men rather
far apart, he at Tenth Street and I at Seventieth, and
with our colds and other disabilities we did not see
each other often. He expected me to come to him, and
I would not without some return of my visits, but we
never ceased to be friends, and good friends, so far as
I know. I joked him once as to how I was going to
come out in his autobiography, and he gave me some
sort of joking reassurance. There was one incident,
however, that brought us very frequently and actively
together. He came one Sunday afternoon to have me
call with him on Maxim Gorky, who was staying at
a hotel a few streets above mine. We were both interested in Gorky, Clemens rather more as a revolutionist
and I as a realist, though I too wished the Russian
Tsar ill, and the novelist well in his mission to the
Russian sympathizers in this republic. But I had lived

through the episode of Kossuth's visit to us and his vain endeavor to raise funds for the Hungarian cause in 1851, when we were a younger and nobler nation than now, with hearts if not hands opener to the " oppressed of Europe "; the oppressed of America, the four or five millions of slaves, we did not count. I did not believe that Gorky could get the money for the cause of freedom in Russia which he had come to get; as I told a valued friend of his and mine, I did not believe he could get twenty-five hundred dollars, and I think now I set the figure too high. I had already refused to sign the sort of general appeal his friends were making to our principles and pockets because I felt it so wholly idle, and when the paper was produced in Gorky's presence and Clemens put his name to it I still refused. The next day Gorky was expelled from his hotel with the woman who was not his wife, but who, I am bound to say, did not look as if she were not, at least to me, who am, however, not versed in those aspects of human nature.

I might have escaped unnoted, but Clemens's familiar head gave us away to the reporters waiting at the elevator's mouth for all who went to see Gorky. As it was, a hunt of interviewers ensued for us severally and jointly. I could remain aloof in my hotel apartment, returning answer to such guardians of the public right to know everything that I had nothing to say of Gorky's domestic affairs; for the public interest had now strayed far from the revolution, and centred entirely upon these. But with Clemens it was different; he lived in a house with a street door kept by a single butler, and he was constantly rung for. I forget how long the siege lasted, but long enough for us to have fun with it. That was the moment of the great Vesuvian eruption, and we figured ourselves in

easy reach of a volcano which was every now and then
" blowing a cone off," as the telegraphic phrase was.
The roof of the great market in Naples had just broken
in under its load of ashes and cinders, and crushed
hundreds of people; and we asked each other if we were
not sorry we had not been there, where the pressure
would have been far less terrific than it was with us
in Fifth Avenue. The forbidden butler came up with
a message that there were some gentlemen below who
wanted to see Clemens.

" How many?" he demanded.

" Five," the butler faltered.

" Reporters?"

The butler feigned uncertainty.

" What would you do?" he asked me.

" I wouldn't see them," I said, and then Clemens
went directly down to them. How or by what means
he appeased their voracity I cannot say, but I fancy
it was by the confession of the exact truth, which was
harmless enough. They went away joyfully, and he
came back in radiant satisfaction with having seen
them. Of course he was right and I wrong, and he
was right as to the point at issue between Gorky and
those who had helplessly treated him with such cruel
ignominy. In America it is not the convention for
men to live openly in hotels with women who are not
their wives. Gorky had violated this convention and
he had to pay the penalty; and concerning the destruction of his efficiency as an emissary of the revolution,
his blunder was worse than a crime.

XXV

To the period of Clemens's residence in Fifth Avenue belongs his efflorescence in white serge. He was always rather aggressively indifferent about dress, and at a very early date in our acquaintance Aldrich and I attempted his reform by clubbing to buy him a cravat. But he would not put away his stiff little black bow, and until he imagined the suit of white serge, he wore always a suit of black serge, truly deplorable in the cut of the sagging frock. After his measure had once been taken he refused to make his clothes the occasion of personal interviews with his tailor; he sent the stuff by the kind elderly woman who had been in the service of the family from the earliest days of his marriage, and accepted the result without criticism. But the white serge was an inspiration which few men would have had the courage to act upon. The first time I saw him wear it was at the authors' hearing before the Congressional Committee on Copyright in Washington. Nothing could have been more dramatic than the gesture with which he flung off his long loose overcoat, and stood forth in white from his feet to the crown of his silvery head. It was a magnificent *coup,* and he dearly loved a *coup;* but the magnificent speech which he made, tearing to shreds the venerable farrago of nonsense about non-property in ideas which had formed the basis of all copyright legislation, made you forget even his spectacularity.

It is well known how proud he was of his Oxford gown, not merely because it symbolized the honor in which he was held by the highest literary body in the world, but because it was so rich and so beautiful. The red and the lavender of the cloth flattered his eyes as the silken black of the same degree of Doctor of Letters, given him years before at Yale, could not do. His frank, defiant happiness in it, mixed with a due sense of burlesque, was something that those lacking his poet-soul could never imagine; they accounted it vain, weak; but that would not have mattered to him if he had known it. In his London sojourn he had formed the top-hat habit, and for a while he lounged splendidly up and down Fifth Avenue in that society emblem; but he seemed to tire of it, and to return kindly to the soft hat of his Southwestern tradition.

He disliked clubs; I don't know whether he belonged to any in New York, but I never met him in one. As I have told, he himself had formed the Human Race Club, but as he never could get it together it hardly counted. There was to have been a meeting of it the time of my only visit to Stormfield in April of last year; but of three who were to have come I alone came. We got on very well without the absentees, after finding them in the wrong, as usual, and the visit was like those I used to have with him so many years before in Hartford, but there was not the old ferment of subjects. Many things had been discussed and put away for good, but we had our old fondness for nature and for each other, who were so differently parts of it. He showed his absolute content with his house, and that was the greater pleasure for me because it was my son who designed it. The architect had been so fortunate as to be able to plan it where a natural avenue of savins, the close-knit, slender, cypress-like cedars of

New England, led away from the rear of the villa to the little level of a pergola, meant some day to be wreathed and roofed with vines. But in the early spring days all the landscape was in the beautiful nakedness of the northern winter. It opened in the surpassing loveliness of wooded and meadowed uplands, under skies that were the first days blue, and the last gray over a rainy and then a snowy floor. We walked up and down, up and down, between the villa terrace and the pergola, and talked with the melancholy amusement, the sad tolerance of age for the sort of men and things that used to excite us or enrage us; now we were far past turbulence or anger. Once we took a walk together across the yellow pastures to a chasmal creek on his grounds, where the ice still knit the clayey banks together like crystal mosses; and the stream far down clashed through and over the stones and the shards of ice. Clemens pointed out the scenery he had bought to give himself elbow-room, and showed me the lot he was going to have me build on. The next day we came again with the geologist he had asked up to Stormfield to analyze its rocks. Truly he loved the place, though he had been so weary of change and so indifferent to it that he never saw it till he came to live in it. He left it all to the architect whom he had known from a child in the intimacy which bound our families together, though we bodily lived far enough apart. I loved his little ones and he was sweet to mine and was their delighted-in and wondered-at friend. Once and once again, and yet again and again, the black shadow that shall never be lifted where it falls, fell in his house and in mine, during the forty years and more that we were friends, and endeared us the more to each other.

XXVI

My visit at Stormfield came to an end with tender relucting on his part and on mine. Every morning before I dressed I heard him sounding my name through the house for the fun of it and I know for the fondness; and if I looked out of my door, there he was in his long nightgown swaying up and down the corridor, and wagging his great white head like a boy that leaves his bed and comes out in the hope of frolic with some one. The last morning a soft sugar-snow had fallen and was falling, and I drove through it down to the station in the carriage which had been given him by his wife's father when they were first married, and been kept all those intervening years in honorable retirement for this final use. Its springs had not grown yielding with time; it had rather the stiffness and severity of age; but for him it must have swung low like the sweet chariot of the negro " spiritual " which I heard him sing with such fervor, when those wonderful hymns of the slaves began to make their way northward. *Go Down, Daniel,* was one in which I can hear his quavering tenor now. He was a lover of the things he liked, and full of a passion for them which satisfied itself in reading them matchlessly aloud. No one could read *Uncle Remus* like him; his voice echoed the voices of the negro nurses who told his childhood the wonderful tales. I remember especially his rapture with Mr. Cable's *Old Creole Days,* and the thrilling force with which he gave the forbidding of the leper's brother when the city's survey ran the course of an avenue through the cottage where the leper lived in hiding: " Strit must not pass!"

Out of a nature rich and fertile beyond any I have known, the material given him by the Mystery that makes a man and then leaves him to make himself over, he wrought a character of high nobility upon a foundation of clear and solid truth. At the last day he will not have to confess anything, for all his life was the free knowledge of any one who would ask him of it. The Searcher of hearts will not bring him to shame at that day, for he did not try to hide any of the things for which he was often so bitterly sorry. He knew where the Responsibility lay, and he took a man's share of it bravely; but not the less fearlessly he left the rest of the answer to the God who had imagined men.

It is in vain that I try to give a notion of the intensity with which he pierced to the heart of life, and the breadth of vision with which he compassed the whole world, and tried for the reason of things, and then left trying. We had other meetings, insignificantly sad and brief; but the last time I saw him alive was made memorable to me by the kind, clear judicial sense with which he explained and justified the labor-unions as the sole present help of the weak against the strong.

Next I saw him dead, lying in his coffin amid those flowers with which we garland our despair in that pitiless hour. After the voice of his old friend Twichell had been lifted in the prayer which it wailed through in broken-hearted supplication, I looked a moment at the face I knew so well; and it was patient with the patience I had so often seen in it: something of puzzle, a great silent dignity, an assent to what must be from the depths of a nature whose tragical seriousness broke in the laughter which the unwise took for the whole of him. Emerson, Longfellow, Lowell, Holmes—I knew them all and all the rest of our sages, poets, seers, critics, humorists; they were like one another and like other literary men; but Clemens was sole, incomparable, the Lincoln of our literature.

MARK TWAIN, 1878

PART SECOND

CRITICISMS

INTRODUCTION

THESE reviews of Mark Twain's books are allowed to follow here in the order of their original publication, with no sort of correction or effort to reconcile them with one another. The reader will find that the critic repeats himself a good deal and reiterates his impressions and opinions of the author, but I hope that he will find an increasing simplicity and modesty in them. My own feeling is that they begin rather stiffly, pedantically, and patronizingly, but that they grow suppler, wiser, and more diffident as they go on. Perhaps I flatter myself in this belief; but I leave that question, together with the reviews themselves, entirely to the reader without further delay.

MARK TWAIN'S FINAL HOME—"STORMFIELD," REDDING, CONNECTICUT

"THE INNOCENTS ABROAD"

(From the "Atlantic Monthly," December, 1869)

THE character of American humor, and its want of resemblance to the humor of Kamtschatka and Patagonia—will the reader forgive us if we fail to set down here the thoughts suggested by these fresh and apposite topics? Will he credit us with a self-denial proportioned to the vastness of Mr. Clemens's very amusing book if we spare to state why he is so droll or—which is as much to the purpose — why we do not know? This reticence will leave us very little to say by way of analysis; and, indeed, there is very little to say of *The Innocents Abroad* which is not of the most obvious and easy description. The idea of a steamer-load of Americans going on a prolonged picnic to Europe and the Holy Land is itself almost sufficiently delightful, and it is perhaps praise enough for the author to add that it suffers nothing from his handling. If one considers the fun of making a volume of six hundred octavo pages upon this subject, in compliance with one of the main conditions of a subscription book's success, bigness namely, one has a tolerably fair piece of humor without troubling Mr. Clemens further. It is out of the bounty and abundance of his own nature that he is as amusing in the execution as in the conception of his work. And it is always good-humored humor, too, that he lavishes on his reader, and even in its impudence it is charming; we do not remember where it is indulged at the cost of the weak or helpless side, or where it is insolent, with all its sauciness and irreverence. The standard shams of travel which everybody sees through suffer possibly more than they ought, but not so much as they might; and one readily forgives the harsh treatment of them in consideration of the novel piece of justice done on such a traveller as suffers under the pseudonym of Grimes. It is impossible also that the quality of humor should not sometimes be strained in the course of so long a narrative; but the wonder is rather in the fact that it is strained so seldom.

Mr. Clemens gets a good deal of his fun out of his fellow-passengers, whom he makes us know pretty well, whether he presents them somewhat caricatured, as in the case of the " Oracle " of the ship, or carefully and exactly done, as in the case of such a shrewd, droll, business-like, sensible, kindly type of the American young man as " Dan." We must say also that the artist who has so copiously illustrated the volume has nearly always helped the author in the portraiture of his fellow-passengers, instead of hurting him, which is saying a good deal for an artist; in fact, we may go further and apply the commendation to all the illustrations; and this in spite of the variety of figures in which the same persons are represented, and the artist's tendency to show the characters on mules where the author says they rode horseback.

Of course, the instructive portions of Mr. Clemens's book are of a general rather than particular character, and the reader gets as travel very little besides series of personal adventures and impressions; he is taught next to nothing about the population of the cities and the character of the rocks in the different localities. Yet the man who can be honest enough to let himself see the realities of human life everywhere, or who has only seen Americans as they are abroad, has not travelled in vain and is far from a useless guide. The very young American who told the English officers that a couple of our gunboats could come and knock Gibraltar into the Mediterranean Sea; the American who at a French restaurant " talked very loudly and coarsely; and laughed boisterously, where all others were so quiet and well behaved," and who ordered " wine, sir!" adding, to raise admiration in a country where wine is as much a matter of course as soup, " I never dine without wine, sir "; the American who had to be addressed several times as Gordon, being so accustomed to hear the name pronounced Gorrdong, and who had forgotten most English words during a three months' sojourn in Paris; the Americans who pitilessly made a three days' journey in Palestine within two days, cruelly overworking the poor beasts they rode, and over-taxing the strength of their comrades in order not to break the Sabbath; the American Pilgrims who travelled half round the world to be able to take a sail on the Sea of Galilee, and then missed their sole opportunity because they required the boatman to take them for one napoleon when he wanted two;—these are all Americans who are painted to peculiar advantage by Mr. Clemens, and who will be easily recognized by such as have had the good-fortune to meet them abroad.

The didactic, however, is not Mr. Clemens's prevailing mood, nor his best, by any means. The greater part of his book is in the vein of irony, which, with a delicious impudence, he attributes to Saint Luke, declaring that Luke, in speaking of the winding " street, called Straight" in Damascus, "is careful not to commit himself; he does not say it is the street which *is* straight, but the 'street which is *called* Straight.' It is a fine piece of irony; it is the only facetious remark in the Bible, I believe." At Tiberias our author saw the women who wear their dowry in their head-dresses of coins. "Most of these maidens were not wealthy, but some few have been kindly dealt with by fortune. I saw heiresses there, worth, in their own right—worth, well, I suppose I might venture to say as much as nine dollars and a half. But such cases are rare. When you come across one of these she naturally puts on airs." He thinks the owner of the horse "Jericho," on which he travelled toward Jerusalem, "had a wrong opinion about him. He had an idea that he was one of those fiery, untamed steeds, but he is not of that character. I know the Arab had this idea, because when he brought the horse out for inspection in Beirout he kept jerking at the bridle and shouting in Arabic, 'Ho! will you? Do you want to run away, you ferocious beast, and break your neck?' when all the time the horse was not doing anything in the world, and only looked like he wanted to lean up against something and think. Whenever he is not shying at things or reaching after a fly he wants to do that yet. How it would surprise his owner to know this!" In this vein of ironical drollery is that now celebrated passage in which Mr. Clemens states that he was affected to tears on coming, a stranger in a strange land, upon the grave of a blood-relation—the tomb of Adam; but that passage is somewhat more studied in tone than most parts of the book, which are written with a very successful approach in style to colloquial drolling. As Mr. Clemens writes of his experiences, we imagine he would talk of them; and very amusing talk it would be: often not at all fine in matter or manner, but full of touches of humor—which if not delicate are nearly always easy—and having a base of excellent sense and good feeling. There is an amount of pure human nature in the book that rarely gets into literature; the depths of our poor unregeneracy—dubious even of the blissfulness of bliss—are sounded by such a simple confession as Mr. Clemens makes in telling of his visit to the Emperor of Russia: " I would as soon have thought of being cheerful in Abraham's bosom as in the palace of an emperor." Almost any topic, and any event of the author's past life, he finds pertinent to the story of European and Oriental travel, and, if the reader finds it impertinent, he does not find it the less amusing. The effect is dependent in so great degree upon this continuous incoherence that no chosen passage can illustrate the spirit of the whole, while the passage itself loses half in separation from the context. Nevertheless, here is part of the account given by Mr. Clemens of the Pilgrims' excursion to the River Jordan, over roads supposed to be infested by Bedouins; and the reader who does not think it droll as it stands can go to our author for the rest:

" I think we must all have determined upon the same line of tactics, for it did seem as if we never would get to Jericho. I had a notoriously slow horse; but somehow I could not keep him in the rear to save my neck. He was forever turning up in the lead. In such cases I trembled a little and got down to fix my saddle. But it was not of any use. The others all got down to fix their saddles, too. I never saw such a time with saddles. It was the first time any of them had got out of order in three weeks, and now they had all broken down at once. I tried walking for exercise—I had not had enough in Jerusalem, searching for holy places.

But it was a failure. The whole mob were suffering for exercise, and it was not fifteen minutes till they were all on foot, and I had the lead again. . . . We were moping along down through this dreadful place, every man in the rear. Our guards, two gorgeous young Arab sheiks, with cargoes of swords, guns, pistols, and daggers on board, were loafing ahead. ' Bedouins!' Every man shrunk up and disappeared in his clothes like a mud-turtle. My first impulse was to dash forward and destroy the Bedouins. My second was to dash to the rear to see if there were any coming in that direction. I acted on the latter impulse. So did all the others. If any Bedouins had approached us then from that point of the compass they would have paid dearly for their rashness."

Under his *nom de plume* of Mark Twain, Mr. Clemens is well known to the very large world of newspaper readers; and this book ought to secure him something better than the uncertain standing of a popular favorite. It is no business of ours to fix his rank among the humorists California has given us, but we think he is, in an entirely different way from all the others, quite worthy of the company of the best.

II

"ROUGHING IT"

(From the "Atlantic Monthly," June, 1872)

WE can fancy the reader of Mr. Clemens's book finding at the end of it (and its six hundred pages of fun are none too many) that, while he has been merely enjoying himself, as he supposes, he has been surreptitiously acquiring a better idea of the flush times in Nevada, and of the adventurous life generally of the recent West, than he could possibly have got elsewhere. The grotesque exaggeration and broad irony with which the life is described are conjecturably the truest colors that could have been used, for all existence there must have looked like an extravagant joke, the humor of which was only deepened by its nether-side of tragedy. The plan of the book is very simple indeed, for it is merely the personal history of Mr. Clemens during a certain number of years, in which he crossed the Plains in the overland stage to Carson City, to be private secretary to the Secretary of Nevada; took the silver-mining fever, and with a friend struck " a blind lead " worth millions; lost it by failing to comply with the mining laws; became local reporter to a Virginia City newspaper; went to San Francisco and suffered extreme poverty in the cause of abstract literature and elegant leisure; was sent to the Sandwich Islands as newspaper correspondent; returned to California and began lecturing and that career of humorist which we should all be sorry to have ended. The " moral " which the author draws from the whole is: " If you are of any account, stay at home and make your way by faithful diligence; but if you are of ' no account ' go away from home, and then you will *have* to work whether you want to or not."

A thousand anecdotes, relevant and irrelevant, embroider the work; excursions and digressions of all kinds are the very woof of it, as it were; everything far-fetched or near at hand is interwoven, and yet the complex is a sort of " harmony of colors " which is not less than triumphant. The stage-drivers and desperadoes of the Plains; the Mormons and their city; the capital of Nevada, and its government and people; the mines and miners; the social, speculative, and financial life of Virginia City; the climate and characteristics of San Francisco; the amusing and startling traits of Sandwich Island civilization—appear in kaleidoscopic succession. Probably an encyclopædia could not be constructed from the book; the work of a human being, it is not unbrokenly nor infallibly funny; nor is it to be always praised for all the literary virtues; but it is singularly entertaining, and its humor is always amiable, manly, and generous.

III

THE PLAY FROM "THE GILDED AGE"

(From the "Atlantic Monthly," June, 1875)

WHOEVER failed to see Mr. Raymond in Mr. Clemens's (Mark Twain's) play of " The Gilded Age," during the recent season at the Globe Theatre, missed a great pleasure. In this drama a player last year almost unknown takes rank at once with the masters of his art, and adds another to the group of realistic actors whom we shall be slow to believe less fine than the finest who have charmed the theatre-going world. One must hereafter name Mr. John T. Raymond in Colonel Sellers with Sothern in " Lord Dundreary," with Jefferson in " Rip Van Winkle," with Salvini in " La Morte Civile," with Fechter in " Hamlet." Like them he does not merely represent; he becomes, he impersonates, the character he plays. The effect is instant; he is almost never Raymond from the moment he steps upon the stage till he leaves it. His assumption of Sellers is so perfect that at some regrettable points where Colonel Sellers pushes matters a little beyond (as where he comments to Laura Hawkins on the beauty of the speech her attorney is making in her defence), we found ourselves wishing that Sellers—not Mr. Raymond—would not overdo it in that way.

The readers of Messrs. Clemens's and Warner's novel

of *The Gilded Age* will easily recall Colonel Sellers, who in the drama is the same character as in the book. The action of the piece has scarcely anything to do with him, and yet, as it happens, it is his constant opportunity to make all his qualities felt. It is scarcely more than a sketch, a framework almost as naked as that which the Italians used to clothe on with their *commedia d' arte;* and it is as unlike good literature as many other excellent acting-plays. Yet any one who should judge it from the literary standpoint, and not with an artistic sense greater and more than literary, would misjudge it. The play is true, in its broad way, to American conditions, and is a fair and just satire upon our generally recognized social and political corruptions. The story is simply that of the good old Tennessee farmer and his wife who come to Missouri at the invitation of Colonel Sellers, and through his speculative friendship lose everything but the farm on the barren knobs in East Tennessee, which they had not sold. Their adopted daughter, a beautiful and ambitious girl, is deceived into marriage with an ex-Confederate officer who has another wife at New Orleans, and they are in the lowest misery when Colonel Sellers (an ex-rebel, who goes in for " the Old Flag— *and* an appropriation ") conceives his great idea that Congress shall buy the Hawkins farm in East Tennessee, and found a freedman's university on it. Laura's beauty is believed to be essential to the success of the bill in Congress, and she and her adoptive sister go to Washington to visit the family of Senator Dilworthy, who is engineering the appropriation. There, one day, Laura is met and insultingly renounced by her betrayer, who tells her that he is a gentleman born, and, even if his wife were not living, would never marry her. She shoots him dead, and the

116

play closes with her trial and acquittal, and the presumed failure of Senator Dilworthy's bill. It is merely an episode, but it is strong and new to the stage, however stale to fact, and it appeals to the spectator's imagination so successfully throughout that he does not mind how very sketchy an episode it is. The betrayer of Laura Hawkins is necessarily a little cheap—betrayers always are—but the rest of the character-material is simple, natural, and good, and in the play the Western quality of the people is always clearly accented without ever being overcharged; they are of the quarter of the world to which all things are still possible, and Sellers is but the highest expression of the hopeful and confiding mood in which they exist. The delightfulness of his disasters consists in the ardor with which he rises above them and enters into a new and more glorious speculation, which even as he talks of it becomes just a *side* speculation—" to keep your money moving "—while his mind develops a yet larger scheme. If he wrecks the fortunes of his friends, it is out of pure zeal and love for them, and he is always ready to share the last dollar with them whether it is his or theirs. Mr. Raymond nicely indicates the shades of the author's intention in his Sellers, and so delicately distinguishes between him and the vulgar, selfish speculator that it is with a sort of remorse one laughs at his dire poverty in the scene where the door drops from the stove and betrays the lighted candle which had imparted a ruddy glow and an apparent warmth from within; or, again, where he makes his friend stay to dine on turnips and water, having first assured himself from his dismayed wife that the water is *good*. The warm, caressing, affectionate nature of the man charms you in Mr. Raymond's performance, and any one who felt the worth of his worthlessness in the novel

117

will feel it the more in the play. It is a personality rarely imagined by the author and interpreted without loss by the actor. Only one point we must except, and we suspect it is not the author's lapse; that is where the Colonel borrows ten dollars of Clay Hawkins, and, being asked not to mention the return of it, stops on his way out and with a glance of low cunning at the audience says, "Well, I won't!" This is thoroughly false and bad, and the stupid laugh it raises ought to make Mr. Raymond ashamed. Colonel Sellers is always serious, and apart from what he considers his legitimate designs upon the public purse is as high-souled and chivalrous as Don Quixote.

Some extremely good suggestions give the ease and composure with which these Missourian ex-slaveholders adapt themselves to the splendors of Washington: once the first people in their own neighborhood, they are of the first people anywhere, and in arriving at luxury they have merely come into their own. But the greatest scenes are in that last act, where Colonel Sellers appears as witness for the defence of Laura Hawkins: as he mounts the stand he affably recognizes and shakes hands with several acquaintances among the jury; he delivers his testimony in the form of a stump speech; he helplessly overrides all the protests, exceptions, and interruptions of the prosecution; from time to time he irresistibly turns and addresses the jury, and can scarcely be silenced; while the attorneys are wrangling together he has seized a juryman by the coat-lapel and is earnestly exhorting him in whisper. The effect is irresistibly ludicrous. It is farce and not farce, for, however extravagantly improbable the situation is, the man in it is deliciously true to himself. There is one bit of pathos, where Sellers tells how he knew Laura as a little girl, and implies that, though she might have killed a man, she could *not* have done *murder,* which is of great value; if Mr. Clemens or Mr. Raymond could work this vein further it would be an immense gain for the piece; Sellers is not a mere glare of absurdity; you do not want to be laughing at him *all* the time; and Mr. Raymond might trust the sympathy of his audience in showing all the tenderness of the man's heart. We are loath to believe that he is not himself equal to showing it.

IV

MARK TWAIN'S "SKETCHES, OLD AND NEW"

(From the "Atlantic Monthly," December, 1875)

IT is easy to say that these new and old sketches by Mr. Clemens are of varying merit; but which, honest reader, would you leave out of the book? There is none but saves itself either by its humor or by the sound sense which it is based on, so that, if one came to reject the flimsiest trifle, one would find it on consideration rather too good to throw away. In reading the book you go through a critical process imaginably very like the author's in editing it; about certain things there can be no question from the first, and you end by accepting all, while you feel that any one else may have his proper doubts about some of the sketches.

The characteristic traits of our friend—he is the friend of mankind—are all here; here is the fine, forecasting humor, starting so far back from its effect that one, knowing some joke must be coming, feels that nothing less than a prophetic instinct can sustain the humorist in its development; here is the burlesque, that seems such plain and simple fun at first, doubling and turning upon itself till you wonder why Mr. Clemens has ever been left out of the list of our *subtile* humorists; here is that peculiar extravagance of statement which we share with all sufficiently elbow-roomed, unneighbored people, but which our English cousins are so good as to consider the distinguishing mark of American humor; here is the incorruptible right-mindedness that always warms the heart to this wit; here is the " dryness," the " breadth "—all the things that so weary us in the praises of him and that so take us with delight in the reading of him. But there is another quality in this book which we fancy we shall hereafter associate more and more with our familiar impressions of him, and that is a growing seriousness of meaning in the apparently unmoralized drolling, which must result from the humorist's second thought of political and social absurdities. It came to Dickens, but the character of his genius was too intensely theatrical to let him make anything but rather poor melodrama of it; to Thackeray, whom our humorists at their best are all like, it came too, and would not suffer him to leave anything, however grotesque, merely laughed at. We shall be disappointed if in Mr. Clemens's case it finds only some desultory expression, like " Lionizing Murderers " and " A New Crime," though there could not be more effective irony than these sketches so far as they go. The first is a very characteristic bit of the humorist's art; and the reader is not so much troubled to find where the laugh comes in as to find where it goes out—for ten to one he is in a sober mind when he is done. The other is more direct satire, but is quite as subtle in its way of presenting those cases in which murderers have been found opportunely insane and acquitted, and gravely sandwiching among them instances in which obviously mad people have been hanged by the same admirable system.

Nothing more final has been thought of on the subject of a great public, statutory wrong than Mark Twain's petition to Congress asking that all property shall be held during the period of forty-two years, or for just so long as an author is permitted to claim copyright in his book. The whole sense and justice applicable to the matter are enforced in this ironical prayer, and there is no argument that could stand against it. If property in houses or lands—which a man may get by dishonest trickery, or usury, or hard rapacity—were in danger of ceasing after forty-two years, the whole virtuous community would rouse itself to perpetuate the author's right to the product of his brain, and no griping bidder at tax-sales but would demand the protection of literature by indefinite copyright. The difficulty is to condition the safety of real estate in this way; but Mark Twain's petition is a move in the right direction.

We should be sorry to give our readers the impression that they are unconsciously to imbibe political and social wisdom from every page of Mr. Clemens's new book, when we merely wished to point out one of his tendencies. Though there is nearly always sense in his nonsense, yet he is master of the art of pure drolling. The grotesque cannot go further than in that mediæval romance of his where he is obliged to abandon his hero or heroine at the most critical moment simply because he can see no way to get him or her out of the difficulty; and there is a delicious novelty in that ghost-story where the unhappy spectre of the Cardiff Giant is mortified to find that he has been haunting a plaster cast of himself in New York, while his stone original was lying in Albany. "The Experiences of the McWilliamses with the Membranous Croup" is a bit of *genre* romance which must read like an abuse of confidence to every husband and father. These are among the new sketches, though none of them have staled by custom, and the old sketches are to be called so merely for contradistinction's sake. "How I Once Edited an Agricultural Paper," "About Barbers," "Cannibalism in the Cars," "The Undertaker's Chat," "The Scriptural Panoramist," "To Raise Poultry," "A Visit to Niagara" are all familiar favorites, which, when we have read them, we wish merely to have the high privilege of immediately reading over again. We must not leave the famous "Jumping Frog" out of their honorable and pleasant company; it is here in a new effect, first as the "Jumping Frog" in Mark Twain's original English, then in the French of the *Revue des Deux Mondes,* and then in his literal version of the French, which he gives that the reader may see how his frog has been made to appear "to the distorted French eye."

But by far the most perfect piece of work in the book is "A True Story," which resulted, we remember, in some confusion of the average critical mind when it was first published in these pages a little more than one year ago. It is simply the story an old black cook tells of how her children were all sold away from her, and how after twenty years she found her youngest boy again. The shyness of an enlightened and independent press respecting this history was something extremely amusing to see, and one could fancy it a spectacle of delightful interest to the author if it had not had such disheartening features. Mostly the story was described in the notices of the magazine as a humorous sketch by Mark Twain; sometimes it was mentioned as a paper apparently out of the author's usual line; again it was handled non-committally as one of Mark Twain's extravagances. Evidently the critical mind feared a lurking joke. Not above two or three notices out of hundreds recognized "A True Story" for what it was—namely, a study of character as true as life itself, strong, tender, and most movingly pathetic in its

perfect fidelity to the tragic fact. We beg the reader
to turn to it again in this book. We can assure him
that he has a great surprise and a strong emotion in
store for him. The rugged truth of the sketch leaves
all other stories of slave life infinitely far behind, and
reveals a gift in the author for the simple, dramatic
report of reality which we have seen equalled in no
other American writer.

V

"THE ADVENTURES OF TOM SAWYER"

(From the "Atlantic Monthly," December, 1875)

Mr. Aldrich has studied the life of *A Bad Boy* as
the pleasant reprobate led it in a quiet old New England town twenty-five or thirty years ago, where in
spite of the natural outlawry of boyhood he was more
or less part of a settled order of things, and was hem-
med in, to some measure, by the traditions of an established civilization. Mr. Clemens, on the contrary, has
taken the boy of the Southwest for the hero of his
new book, and has presented him with a fidelity to
circumstance which loses no charm by being realistic
in the highest degree, and which gives incomparably
the best picture of life in that region as yet known to
fiction. The town where Tom Sawyer was born and
brought up is some such idle, shabby little Mississippi
River town as Mr. Clemens has so well described in
his piloting reminiscences, but Tom belongs to the better sort of people in it, and has been bred to fear God
and dread the Sunday-school according to the strictest
rite of the faiths that have characterized all the respec-
tability of the West. His subjection in these respects
does not so deeply affect his inherent tendencies but
that he makes himself a beloved burden to the poor,
tender-hearted old aunt who brings him up with his

orphan brother and sister, and struggles vainly with
his manifold sins, actual and imaginary. The limitations of his transgressions are nicely and artistically
traced. He is mischievous, but not vicious; he is ready
for almost any depredation that involves the danger
and honor of adventure, but profanity he knows may
provoke a thunderbolt upon the heart of the blasphemer,
and he almost never swears; he resorts to any stratagem
to keep out of school, but he is not a downright liar,
except upon terms of after shame and remorse that
make his falsehood bitter to him. He is cruel, as all
children are, but chiefly because he is ignorant; he is
not mean, but there are very definite bounds to his
generosity; and his courage is the Indian sort, full of
prudence and mindful of retreat as one of the conditions of prolonged hostilities. In a word, he is a boy,
and merely and exactly an ordinary boy on the moral
side. What makes him delightful to the reader is that
on the imaginative side he is very much more, and
though every boy has wild and fantastic dreams, this
boy cannot rest till he has somehow realized them.
Till he has actually run off with two other boys in the
character of buccaneer, and lived for a week on an island
in the Mississippi, he has lived in vain; and this passage is but the prelude to more thrilling adventures,
in which he finds hidden treasures, traces the bandits
to their cave, and is himself lost in its recesses. The
local material and the incidents with which his career
is worked up are excellent, and throughout there is
scrupulous regard for the boy's point of view in reference to his surroundings and himself, which shows how
rapidly Mr. Clemens has grown as an artist. We do
not remember anything in which this propriety is violated, and its preservation adds immensely to the grown-
up reader's satisfaction in the amusing and exciting

story. There is a boy's love - affair, but it is never treated otherwise than as a boy's love-affair. When the half-breed has murdered the young doctor, Tom and his friend, Huckleberry Finn, are really, in their boyish terror and superstition, going to let the poor old town-drunkard be hanged for the crime till the terror of that becomes unendurable. The story is a wonderful study of the boy-mind, which inhabits a world quite distinct from that in which he is bodily present with his elders, and in this lies its great charm and its universality, for boy nature, however human nature varies, is the same everywhere.

The tale is very dramatically wrought, and the subordinate characters are treated with the same graphic force that sets Tom alive before us. The worthless vagabond, Huck Finn, is entirely delightful throughout, and in his promised reform his identity is respected: he will lead a decent life in order that he may one day be thought worthy to become a member of that gang of robbers which Tom is to organize. Tom's aunt is excellent, with her kind heart's sorrow and secret pride in Tom; and so is his sister Mary, one of those good girls who are born to usefulness and charity and forbearance and unvarying rectitude. Many village people and local notables are introduced in well-conceived character; the whole little town lives in the reader's sense, with its religiousness, its lawlessness, its droll social distinctions, its civilization qualified by its slaveholding, and its traditions of the wilder West which has passed away. The picture will be instructive to those who have fancied the whole Southwest a sort of vast Pike County, and have not conceived of a sober and serious and orderly contrast to the sort of life that has come to represent the Southwest in literature. Mr. William M. Baker gives a notion of this in his stories,

127

and Mr. Clemens has again enforced the fact here in a book full of entertaining character and of the greatest artistic sincerity.

Tom Brown and Tom Bailey are, among boys in books, alone deserving to be named with Tom Sawyer.

VI

"A TRAMP ABROAD"

(From the "Atlantic Monthly," May, 1880)

IN the natural disgust of a creative mind for the following that vulgarizes and cheapens its work, Mr. Tennyson spoke in parable concerning his verse:

> "Most can raise the flower now,
>   For all have got the seed.
> And some are pretty enough,
>   And some are poor indeed;
> And now again the people
>   Call it but a weed."

But this bad effect is to the final loss of the rash critic rather than the poet, who necessarily survives imitation, and appeals to posterity as singly as if nobody had tried to ape him; while those who rejected him, along with his copyists, have meantime thrown away a great pleasure. Just at present some of us are in danger of doing ourselves a like damage. " Thieves from over the wall " have got the seed of a certain drollery which sprouts and flourishes plentifully in every newspaper, until the thought of American humor is becoming terrible; and sober-minded people are beginning to have serious question whether we are not in danger of degenerating into a nation of wits. But we ought to take courage from observing, as we may, that this plentiful crop of humor is not racy of the original soil; that, in short, the thieves from over the wall were not also able to steal Mr. Clemens's garden-plot. His humor springs from a certain intensity of common sense, a passionate love of justice, and a generous scorn of what is petty and mean; and it is these qualities which his " school " have not been able to " convey." They have never been more conspicuous than in this last book of his, to which they may be said to give its sole coherence. It may be claiming more than a humorist could wish to assert that he is always in earnest; but this strikes us as the paradoxical charm of Mr. Clemens's best humor. Its wildest extravagance is the break and fling from a deep feeling, a wrath with some folly which disquiets him worse than other men, a personal hatred for some humbug or pretension that embitters him beyond anything but laughter. It must be because he is intolerably weary of the twaddle of pedestrianizing that he conceives the notion of a tramp through Europe, which he operates by means of express trains, steamboats, and private carriages, with the help of an agent and a courier; it is because he has a real loathing, otherwise inexpressible, for Alp-climbing that he imagines an ascent of the Riffelberg with " half a mile of men and mules " tied together by rope. One sees that affectations do not first strike him as ludicrous merely, but as detestable. He laughs, certainly, at an abuse, at ill manners, at conceit, at cruelty, and you must laugh with him; but, if you enter into the very spirit of his humor, you feel that if he could set these things right there would be very little laughing. At the bottom of his heart he has often the grimness of a reformer; his wit is turned by preference not upon human nature, not upon droll situations and things abstractly ludicrous, but upon matters that are out of joint, that are unfair or unnecessarily ignoble, and cry out to his love of justice for discipline. Much of the fun is at his own cost where he boldly attempts to grapple with some hoary abuse and gets worsted by it, as in his verbal contest with the girl at the medicinal springs in Baden, who returns " that beggar's answer " of half Europe, " What you please," to his ten-times-repeated demand of " How much?" and gets the last word. But it is plain that if he had his way there would be a fixed price for those waters very suddenly, and without regard to the public amusement or regret for lost opportunities of humorous writing.

It is not Mr. Clemens's business in Europe to find fault, or to contrast things there with things here, to the perpetual disadvantage of that continent; but sometimes he lets homesickness and his disillusion speak. This book has not the fresh frolicsomeness of the *Innocents Abroad;* it is Europe revisited and seen through eyes saddened by much experience of tables d'hôte, old masters, and travelling Americans—whom, by-the-way, Mr. Clemens advises not to travel too long at a time in Europe, lest they lose national feeling and become travelled Americans. Nevertheless, if we have been saying anything about the book or about the sources of Mr. Clemens's humor to lead the reader to suppose that it is not immensely amusing, we have done it a great wrong. It is delicious, whether you open it at the sojourn in Heidelberg, or the voyage down the Neckar on a raft, or the mountaineering in Switzerland, or the excursion beyond Alps into Italy. The method is that discursive method which Mark Twain has led us to expect of him. The story of a man who had a claim against the United States Government is not impertinent to the bridge across the River Reuss;

the remembered tricks played upon a printer's devil in Missouri are the natural concomitants of a walk to Oppenau. The writer has always the unexpected at his command, in small things as well as great: the story of the raft journey on the Neckar is full of these surprises; it is wholly charming. If there is too much of anything, it is that ponderous and multitudinous ascent of the Riffelberg; there is probably too much of that, and we would rather have another appendix in its place. The appendices are all admirable, especially those on the German language and the German newspapers, which get no more sarcasm than they deserve.

One should not rely upon all statements of the narrative, but its spirit is the truth, and it honestly breathes American travel in Europe as a large minority of our forty millions know it. The material is inexhaustible in the mere Americans themselves, and they are rightful prey. Their effect upon Mr. Clemens has been to make him like them best at home; and no doubt most of them will agree with him that " to be condemned to live as the average European family lives would make life a pretty heavy burden to the average American family." This is the sober conclusion which he reaches at last, and it is unquestionable, like the vastly greater part of the conclusions at which he arrives throughout. His opinions are no longer the opinions of the Western American newly amused and disgusted at the European difference, but the Western American's impressions on being a second time confronted with things he has had time to think over. This is the serious undercurrent of the book, to which we find ourselves reverting from its obvious comicality. We have, indeed, so great an interest in Mr. Clemens's likes and dislikes, and so great respect for his preferences generally, that we are loath to let the book go

to our readers without again wishing them to share
these feelings. There is no danger that they will not
laugh enough over it; that is an affair which will take
care of itself; but there is a possibility that they may
not think enough over it. Every account of European
travel or European life by a writer who is worth reading for any reason is something for our reflection and
possible instruction; and in this delightful work of a
man of most original and characteristic genius " the
average American " will find much to enlighten as well
as amuse him, much to comfort and stay him in such
Americanism as is worth having, and nothing to flatter
him in a mistaken national vanity or a stupid national
prejudice.

VII

MARK TWAIN

(From the " Century Magazine," September, 1882)

In one form or other, Mr. Samuel L. Clemens has
told the story of his life in his books, and in sketching
his career I shall have to recur to the leading facts
rather than to offer fresh information. He was remotely of Virginian origin and more remotely of good
English stock; the name was well known before his
time in the South, where a senator, a congressman, and
other dignitaries had worn it; but his branch of the
family fled from the destitution of those vast landed
possessions in Tennessee, celebrated in *The Gilded Age,*
and went very poor to Missouri. Mr. Clemens was
born on November 30, 1835, at Florida in the latter
State, but his father removed shortly afterward to
Hannibal, a small town on the Mississippi, where most
of the humorist's boyhood was spent. Hannibal as a
name is hopelessly confused and ineffective; but if we
can know nothing of Mr. Clemens from Hannibal, we
can know much of Hannibal from Mr. Clemens, who,
in fact, has studied a loafing, out-at-elbows, down-at-the-
heels, slaveholding Mississippi River town of thirty
years ago, with such strong reality in his boy's romance
of *Tom Sawyer,* that we need inquire nothing further
concerning the type. The original perhaps no longer
134

exists anywhere; certainly not in Hannibal, which has grown into a flourishing little city since Mr. Clemens sketched it. In his time the two embattled forces of civilization and barbarism were encamped at Hannibal, as they are at all times and everywhere; the morality of the place was the morality of a slaveholding community: fierce, arrogant, one - sided — this virtue for white, and that for black folks; and the religion was Calvinism in various phases, with its predestinate aristocracy of saints and its rabble of hopeless sinners. Doubtless, young Clemens escaped neither of the opposing influences wholly. His people like the rest were slaveholders; but his father, like so many other slaveholders, abhorred slavery—silently, as he must in such a time and place. If the boy's sense of justice suffered anything of that perversion which so curiously and pitiably maimed the reason of the whole South, it does not appear in his books, where there is not an ungenerous line, but always, on the contrary, a burning resentment of all manner of cruelty and wrong.

The father, an austere and singularly upright man, died bankrupt when Clemens was twelve years old, and the boy had thereafter to make what scramble he could for an education. He got very little learning in school, and like so many other Americans in whom the literary impulse is native, he turned to the local printing-office for some of the advantages from which he was otherwise cut off. Certain records of the three years spent in the Hannibal *Courier* office are to be found in Mark Twain's book of sketches; but I believe there is yet no history anywhere of the *wanderjahre,* in which he followed the life of a jour-printer, from town to town, and from city to city, penetrating even so far into the vague and fabled East as Philadelphia and New York.

He returned to his own town—his *patria*—sated, if not satisfied, with travel, and at seventeen he resolved to "learn the river" from St. Louis to New Orleans as a steamboat pilot. Of this period of his life he has given a full account in the delightful series of papers, *Piloting on the Mississippi,* which he printed seven years ago in the *Atlantic Monthly.* The growth of the railroads and the outbreak of the Civil War put an end to profitable piloting, and at twenty-four he was again open to a vocation. He listened for a moment to the loudly calling drum of that time, and he was actually in camp for three weeks on the rebel side; but the unorganized force to which he belonged was disbanded, and he finally did not "go with his section" either in sentiment or in fact. His brother having been appointed Lieutenant-Governor of Nevada Territory, Mr. Clemens went out with him as his private secretary; but he soon resigned his office and withdrew to the mines. He failed as a miner, in the ordinary sense; but the life of the mining-camp yielded him the wealth that the pockets of the mountain denied; he had the Midas touch without knowing it, and all these grotesque experiences have since turned into gold under his hand. After his failure as a miner had become evident even to himself, he was glad to take the place of local editor on the Virginia City *Enterprise,* a newspaper for which he had amused himself in writing from time to time. He had written for the newspapers before this; few Americans escape that fate; and as an apprentice in the Hannibal *Courier* office his humor had embroiled some of the leading citizens, and impaired the fortunes of that journal by the alienation of several delinquent subscribers.

But it was in the *Enterprise* that he first used his pseudonym of "Mark Twain," which he borrowed from the vernacular of the river, where the man heaving the lead calls out " Mark twain!" instead of " Mark two!" In 1864, he accepted, on the San Francisco *Morning Call,* the same sort of place which he had held on the *Enterprise,* and he soon made his *nom de guerre* familiar " on that coast "; he not only wrote " local items " in the *Call,* but he printed humorous sketches in various periodicals, and, two years later, he was sent to the Sandwich Islands as correspondent of a Sacramento paper.

When he came back he " entered the lecture-field," as it used to be phrased. Of these facts there is, as all English - speaking readers know, full record in *Roughing It,* though I think Mr. Clemens has not mentioned there his association with that extraordinary group of wits and poets, of whom Mr. Bret Harte, Mr. Charles Warren Stoddard, Mr. Charles H. Webb, Mr. Prentice Mulford, were, with himself, the most conspicuous. These ingenious young men, with the fatuity of gifted people, had established a literary newspaper in San Francisco, and they brilliantly co-operated to its early extinction.

In 1867, Mr. Clemens made in the *Quaker City* the excursion to Europe and the East which he has commemorated in *The Innocents Abroad.* Shortly after his return he married, and placed himself at Buffalo, where he bought an interest in one of the city newspapers; later he came to Hartford, where he has since remained, except for the two years spent in a second visit to Europe. The incidents of this visit he has characteristically used in *A Tramp Abroad;* and, in fact, I believe the only book of Mr. Clemens's which is not largely autobiographical is *The Prince and the Pauper:* the scene being laid in England, in the early part of the sixteenth century, the difficulties presented to a nineteenth - century autobiographer were insurmountable.

The habit of putting his own life, not merely in its results but in its processes, into his books, is only one phase of the frankness of Mr. Clemens's humorous attitude. The transparent disguise of the pseudonym once granted him, he asks the reader to grant him nothing else. In this he differs wholly from most other American humorists, who have all found some sort of dramatization of their personality desirable if not necessary. Charles F. Browne, " delicious " as he was when he dealt with us directly, preferred the disguise of " Artemus Ward " the showman; Mr. Locke likes to figure as " Petroleum V. Nasby," the cross-roads politician; Mr. Shaw chooses to masquerade as the saturnine philosopher " Josh Billings "; and each of these humorists appeals to the grotesqueness of misspelling to help out his fun. It was for Mr. Clemens to reconcile the public to humor which contented itself with the established absurdities of English orthography; and I am inclined to attribute to the example of his immense success, the humane spirit which characterizes our recent popular humor. There is still sufficient flippancy and brutality in it; but there is no longer the stupid and monkeyish cruelty of motive and intention which once disgraced and insulted us. Except the political humorists, like Mr. Lowell—if there were any like him —the American humorists formerly chose the wrong in public matters; they were on the side of slavery, of drunkenness, and of irreligion; the friends of civilization were their prey; their spirit was thoroughly vulgar and base. Before " John Phœnix," there was scarcely any American humorist—not of the distinctly literary sort—with whom one could smile and keep one's self-respect. The great Artemus himself was not guiltless;

but the most popular humorist who ever lived has not to accuse himself, so far as I can remember, of having written anything to make one morally ashamed of liking him. One can readily make one's strictures; there is often more than a suggestion of forcing in his humor; sometimes it tends to horse-play; sometimes the extravagance overleaps itself, and falls flat on the other side; but I cannot remember that in Mr. Clemens's books I have ever been asked to join him in laughing at any good or really fine thing. But I do not mean to leave him with this negative praise; I mean to say of him that as Shakespeare, according to Mr. Lowell's saying, was the first to make poetry all poetical, Mark Twain was the first to make humor all humorous. He has not only added more in bulk to the sum of harmless pleasures than any other humorist; but more in the spirit that is easily and wholly enjoyable. There is nothing lost in literary attitude, in labored dictionary funning, in affected quaintness, in dreary dramatization, in artificial " dialect "; Mark Twain's humor is as simple in form and as direct as the statesmanship of Lincoln or the generalship of Grant.

When I think how purely and wholly American it is, I am a little puzzled at its universal acceptance. We are doubtless the most thoroughly homogeneous people that ever existed as a great nation. There is such a parity in the experiences of Americans that Mark Twain or Artemus Ward appeals as unerringly to the consciousness of our fifty millions as Goldoni appealed to that of his hundred thousand Venetians. In our phrase, we have somehow all " been there "; in fact, generally, and in sympathy almost certainly, we have been there. In another generation or two, perhaps, it will be wholly different; but as yet the average American is the man who has risen; he has known poverty, and privation, and low conditions; he has very often known squalor; and now, in his prosperity, he regards the past with a sort of large, pitying amusement; he is not the least ashamed of it; he does not feel that it characterizes him any more than the future does. Our humor springs from this multiform American experience of life, and securely addresses itself—in reminiscence, in phrase, in its whole material—to the intelligence bred of like experience. It is not of a class for a class; it does not employ itself with the absurdities of a tailor as a tailor; its conventions, if it has any, are all new, and of American make. When it mentions hash we smile because we have each somehow known the cheap boarding-house or restaurant; when it alludes to putting up stoves in the fall, each of us feels the grime and rust of the pipes on his hands; the introduction of the lightning-rod man, or the book-agent, establishes our brotherhood with the humorist at once. But how is it with the vast English-speaking world outside of these States, to which hash, and stovepipes, and lightning-rod men and book-agents are as strange as lords and ladies, dungeon-keeps and battlements are to us? Why, in fine, should an English chief-justice keep Mark Twain's books always at hand? Why should Darwin have gone to them for rest and refreshment at midnight when spent with scientific research?

I suppose that Mark Twain transcends all other American humorists in the universal qualities. He deals very little with the pathetic, which he nevertheless knows very well how to manage, as he has shown, notably in the true story of the old slave-mother; but there is a poetic lift in his work, even when he permits you to recognize it only as something satirized. There is always the touch of nature, the presence of a sincere and frank manliness in what he says, the companion-

140

ship of a spirit which is at once delightfully open and deliciously shrewd. Elsewhere I have tried to persuade the reader that his humor is at its best the foamy break of the strong tide of earnestness in him. But it would be limiting him unjustly to describe him as a satirist; and it is hardly practicable to establish him in people's minds as a moralist; he has made them laugh too long; they will not believe him serious; they think some joke is always intended. This is the penalty, as Doctor Holmes has pointed out, of making one's first success as a humorist. There was a paper of Mark Twain's printed in the *Atlantic Monthly* some years ago and called " The Facts Concerning the Late Carnival of Crime in Connecticut," which ought to have won popular recognition of the ethical intelligence underlying his humor. It was, of course, funny; but under the fun it was an impassioned study of the human conscience. Hawthorne or Bunyan might have been proud to imagine that powerful allegory, which had a grotesque force far beyond either of them. It had been read before a literary club in Hartford; a reverend gentleman had offered the author his pulpit for the next Sunday if he would give it as a homily there. Yet it quite failed of the response I had hoped for it, and I shall not insist here upon Mark Twain as a moralist; though I warn the reader that if he leaves out of the account an indignant sense of right and wrong, a scorn of all affectation and pretence, an ardent hate of meanness and injustice, he will come indefinitely short of knowing Mark Twain.

His powers as a story-teller were evident in hundreds of brief sketches before he proved them in *Tom Sawyer* and *The Prince and the Pauper*. Both of these books, aside from their strength of characterization, are fascinating as mere narratives, and I can think of no writer living who has in higher degree the art of interesting his reader from the first word. This is a far rarer gift than we imagine, and I shall not call it a subordinate charm in Mark Twain's books, rich as they otherwise are. I have already had my say about *Tom Sawyer,* whose only fault is an excess of reality in portraying the character and conditions of Southwestern boyhood as it was forty years ago, and which is full of that poetic sympathy with nature and human nature which I always find in Mark Twain. *The Prince and the Pauper* has particularly interested me for the same qualities which, in a study of the past, we call romantic, but which alone can realize the past for us. Occasionally the archaic diction gives way and lets us down hard upon the American parlance of the nineteenth century; but mainly the illusion is admirably sustained, and the tale is to be valued not only in itself, but as an earnest of what Mr. Clemens might do in fiction when he has fairly done with autobiography in its various forms. His invention is of the good old sort, like De Foe's more than that of any other English writer, and like that of the Spanish picaresque novelists, Mendoza and the rest; it flows easily from incident to incident, and does not deepen into situation. In the romance it operates as lightly and unfatiguingly as his memory in the realistic story.

His books abound in passages of dramatic characterization, and he is, as the reader knows, the author of the most successful American play. I believe Mr. Clemens has never claimed the reconstruction of Colonel Sellers for the stage; but he nevertheless made the play, for whatever is good in it came bodily from his share of the novel of *The Gilded Age.* It is a play which succeeds by virtue of the main personage, and this personage, from first to last, is quite outside of the dramatic action, which sometimes serves and sometimes does not serve the purpose of presenting Colonel Sellers. Where the drama fails, Sellers rises superior and takes the floor; and we forget the rest. Mr. Raymond conceived the character wonderfully well, and he plays it with an art that ranks him to that extent with the great actors; but he has in nowise " created " it. If any one " created " Colonel Sellers, it was Mark Twain, as the curious reader may see on turning again to the novel; but I suspect that Colonel Sellers was never created, except as other men are; that he was found somewhere and transferred, living, to the book.

I prefer to speak of Mr. Clemens's artistic qualities because it is to these that his humor will owe its perpetuity. All fashions change, and nothing more wholly and quickly than the fashion of fun; as any one may see by turning back to what amused people in the last generation; that stuff is terrible. As Europe becomes more and more the playground of Americans, and every scene and association becomes insipidly familiar, the jokes about the old masters and the legends will no longer be droll to us. Neither shall we care for the huge Californian mirth, when the surprise of the picturesquely mixed civilization and barbarism of the Pacific Coast has quite died away; and Mark Twain would pass with the conditions that have made him intelligible, if he were not an artist of uncommon power as well as a humorist. He portrays and interprets real types, not only with exquisite appreciation and sympathy, but with a force and truth of drawing that makes them permanent. Artemus Ward was very funny, that can never be denied; but it must be owned that the figure of the literary showman is as wholly factitious as his spelling; the conception is one that has to be constantly humored by the reader. But the innumerable characters sketched by Mark Twain are actualities, however caricatured—and, usually, they are not so very much caricatured. He has brought back the expression of Western humor to sympathy with the sane orthography in John Phœnix; but Mark Twain is vastly more original in form. Derby was weighed upon by literary tradition; he was " academic " at times, but Mr. Clemens is never " academic." There is no drawing from casts; in his work evidently the life has everywhere been studied: and it is his apparent unconsciousness of any other way of saying a thing except the natural way that makes his books so restful and refreshing. Our little nervous literary sensibilities may suffer from his extravagance, or from other traits of his manner, but we have not to beat our breasts at the dread apparition of Dickens's or Thackeray's hand in his page. He is far too honest and sincere a soul for that; and where he is obliged to force a piece of humor to its climax— as sometimes happens—he does not call in his neighbors to help; he does it himself, and is probably sorry that he had to do it.

I suppose that even in so slight and informal a study as this, something like an " analysis " of our author's humor is expected. But I much prefer not to make it. I have observed that analyses of humor are apt to leave one rather serious, and to result in an entire volatilization of the humor. If the prevailing spirit of Mark Twain's humor is not a sort of good-natured self-satire, in which the reader may see his own absurdities reflected, I scarcely should be able to define it.

VIII

"A CONNECTICUT YANKEE IN KING ARTHUR'S COURT"

(From " Harper's Magazine," 1890)

MR. CLEMENS, we call him, rather than Mark Twain, because we feel that in this book our arch-humorist imparts more of his personal quality than in anything else he has done. Here he is to the full the humorist, as we know him; but he is very much more, and his strong, indignant, often infuriate hate of injustice, and his love of equality, burn hot through the manifold adventures and experiences of the tale. What he thought about prescriptive right and wrong, we had partly learned in *The Prince and the Pauper* and in *Huckleberry Finn*, but it is this last book which gives his whole mind. The elastic scheme of the romance allows it to play freely back and forward between the sixth century and the nineteenth century; and often while it is working the reader up to a blasting contempt of monarchy and aristocracy in King Arthur's time, the dates are magically shifted under him, and he is confronted with exactly the same principles in Queen Victoria's time. The delicious satire, the marvellous wit, the wild, free, fantastic humor are the colors of the tapestry, while the texture is a humanity that lives in every fibre. At every moment the scene amuses, but it is all the time an object-lesson in democracy. It makes us glad of our republic and our epoch; but it does not flatter us into a fond content with them; there are passages in which we see that the noble of Arthur's day, who fattened on the blood and sweat of his bondmen, is one in essence with the capitalist of Mr. Harrison's day who grows rich on the labor of his underpaid wagemen. . . .

Mr. Clemens's glimpses of monastic life in Arthur's realm are true enough; and if they are not the whole truth of the matter, one may easily get it in some such book as Mr. Brace's *Gesta Christi,* where the full light of history is thrown upon the transformation of the world, if not the Church, under the influence of Christianity. In the mean time, if any one feels that the justice done the churchmen of King Arthur's time is too much of one kind, let him turn to that heart-breaking scene where the brave monk stands with the mother and her babe on the scaffold, and execrates the hideous law which puts her to death for stealing enough to keep her from starving. It is one of many passages in the story where our civilization of to-day sees itself mirrored in the cruel barbarism of the past, the same in principle and only softened in custom. With shocks of consciousness, one recognizes in such episodes that the laws are still made for the few against the many, and that the preservation of things, not men, is still the ideal of legislation. But we do not wish to leave the reader with the notion that Mr. Clemens's work is otherwise than obliquely serious. Upon the face of it you have a story no more openly didactic than *Don Quixote,* which we found ourselves more than once thinking of as we read, though always with a sense of the kindlier and truer heart of our time. Never once, we believe, has Mark Twain been funny at the cost of the weak, the unfriended, the helpless; and this is rather more than you can say of Cid Hamet ben Engeli. But the two writers are of the same humorous largeness; and when the Connecticut man rides out at dawn, in a suit of Arthurian armor, and gradually heats up under the mounting sun in what he calls "that stove"; and a fly gets between the bars of his visor; and he cannot reach his handkerchief in his helmet to wipe the sweat from his streaming face; and at last when he cannot bear it any longer, and dismounts at the side of a brook, and makes the distressed damsel who has been riding behind him take off his helmet, and fill it with water, and pour gallon after gallon down the collar of his wrought-iron cutaway, you have a situation of as huge a grotesqueness as any that Cervantes conceived.

The distressed damsel is the Lady Corisande; he calls her Sandy, and he is troubled in mind at riding about the country with her in that way; for he is not only very doubtful that there is nothing in the castle where she says there are certain princesses imprisoned and persecuted by certain giants, but he feels that it is not quite nice: he is engaged to a young lady in East Hartford, and he finds Sandy a fearful bore at first, though in the end he loves and marries her, finding that he hopelessly antedates the East Hartford young lady by thirteen centuries. How he gets into King Arthur's realm, the author concerns himself as little as any of us do with the mechanism of our dreams. In fact, the whole story has the lawless operation of a dream; none of its prodigies are accounted for; they take themselves for granted, and neither explain nor justify themselves. Here he is, that Connecticut man, foreman of one of the shops in Colt's pistol factory, and full to the throat of the invention and the self-satisfaction of the nineteenth century, at the court of the mythic Arthur. He is promptly recognized as a being of extraordinary powers and becomes the king's right-hand man, with the title of The Boss; but as he has apparently no lineage or blazon, he has no social standing, and the meanest noble has precedence of him, just as would happen in England to-day. The reader may faintly fancy the consequences flowing from this situation, which he will find so vividly fancied for him in the book; but they are simply irreportable. The scheme confesses allegiance to nothing; the incidents, the facts, follow as they will. The Boss cannot rest from introducing the apparatus of our time, and he tries to impart its spirit with a thousand most astonishing effects. He starts a daily paper in Camelot; he torpedoes a holy well; he blows up a party of insolent knights with a dynamite bomb; when he and the king disguise themselves as peasants, in order to learn the real life of the people, and are taken and sold for slaves, and then sent to the gallows for the murder of their master, Launcelot arrives to their rescue with five hundred knights on bicycles. It all ends with the Boss's proclamation of the Republic after Arthur's death, and his destruction of the whole chivalry of England by electricity.

We can give no proper notion of the measureless play of an imagination which has a gigantic jollity in its feats, together with the tenderest sympathy. There are incidents in this wonder-book which wring the heart for what has been of cruelty and wrong in the past, and leave it burning with shame and hate for the conditions which are of like effect in the present. It is one of its magical properties that the fantastic fable of Arthur's far-off time is also too often the sad truth of ours; and the magician who makes us feel in it that we have just begun to know his power, teaches equality and fraternity in every phase of his phantasmagory.

He leaves, to be sure, little of the romance of the olden time, but no one is more alive to the simple, mostly tragic poetry of it; and we do not remember any book which imparts so clear a sense of what was truly heroic in it. With all his scorn of kingcraft, and all his ireful contempt of caste, no one yet has been fairer to the nobility of character which they cost so much too much to develop. The mainly ridiculous Arthur of Mr. Clemens has his moments of being as fine and high as the Arthur of Lord Tennyson; and the keener light which shows his knights and ladies in their child‑like simplicity and their innocent coarseness throws all their best qualities into relief. This book is in its last effect the most matter-of-fact narrative, for it is always true to human nature, the only truth possible, the only truth essential, to fiction. The humor of the conception and of the performance is simply immense; but more than ever Mr. Clemens's humor seems the sunny break of his intense conviction. We must all recognize him here as first of those who laugh, not merely because his fun is unrivalled, but because there is a force of right feeling and clear thinking in it that never got into fun before, except in *The Bigelow Papers*. Throughout, the text in all its circumstances and meaning is supplemented by the illustrations of an artist who has entered into the wrath and the pathos as well as the fun of the thing, and made them his own.

IX

"JOAN OF ARC"

(From "Harper's Weekly," 1896)

THE historical novel is one of those flexible inventions which can be fitted to the mood or genius of any writer, and can be either story or history in the proportion he prefers. Walter Scott, who contrived it, tested its elasticity as fully as any of the long line of romancers who have followed him in every land and language. It has been a favorite form with readers from the first, and it will be to the last, because it gives them the feeling that to read so much about people who once lived and figured in human events is not such a waste of time as to read of people who never lived at all, or figured in anything but the author's fancy. With a race like ours, which always desires a reason, or at least an excuse, for enjoying itself, this feeling no doubt availed much for fiction, and helped to decide the fate of the novel favorably when its popularity was threatened by the good, stupid Anglo-Saxon conscience. Probably it had the largest share in establishing fiction as a respectable literary form, and in giving it the primacy which it now enjoys. Without the success of the monstrous fables which the gentle Sir Walter palmed off upon his generation in the shape of historical fiction, we should hardly have revered as masters in a beautiful art the writers who have since swayed our emotions. Jane Austen, Miss Edgeworth, Hawthorne, Thackeray, George Eliot, Mr. Henry James, might have sought a hearing from serious persons in vain for the truth that was in them if the historical novel had not established fiction in the respect of our race as a pleasure which might be enjoyed without self-reproach, or as the sugar of a pill which would be none the less powerful in its effects upon the system because it was agreeable to take.

It would be interesting to know, but not very pertinent to inquire, how far our great humorist's use of the historical form in fiction was prompted by love of it, or by an instinctive perception that it was the only form in which he could hope to deliver a message of serious import without being taken altogether in jest. But, at any rate, we can be sure that in each of Mark Twain's attempts of this sort, in the *Prince and the Pauper,* in the *Connecticut Yankee in King Arthur's Court,* and in the *Personal Recollections of Joan of Arc,* he was taken with the imaginative—that is to say, the true—nature of his theme, and that he made this the channel of the rich vein of poetry which runs through all his humor and keeps it sound whether it is grotesque or whether it is pathetic in effect.

The first of these three books is addressed to children, but it is not children who can get the most out of it; the last is offered to the sympathy and intelligence of men and women, and yet I should not be surprised if it made its deepest and most lasting appeal to the generous heart of youth. But I think that the second will remain the enduring consolation of old and young alike, and will be ranged in this respect and as a masterpiece of humor beside the great work of Cervantes. Since the Ingenious Gentleman of La

Mancha there is nothing to compare with the Yankee at the Court of King Arthur, and I shall be very much disappointed in posterity if it does not agree with me. In that colossally amusing scheme, that infinitely suggestive situation, the author was hampered by no such distinct records as he has had to grapple with in his *Personal Recollections of Joan of Arc.* He could launch himself into a realm of fable and turn it into fact by virtue of his own strong and vivid reality, while in a scene whose figures and events are all ascertained by history his fancy has had to work reversely, and transmute the substance into the airy fabric of romance. The result will not be accepted without difficulty by two sorts of critics: the sort who would have had him stick closer to the conventional ideal of the past, as it has been derived from other romancers, and the sort who would have had him throw that altogether away and trust to his own divinations of its life and spirit from the events as set down and from his abundant knowledge of human nature through himself.

I confess that I am of these, and I have the least to complain of, I think. It would be impossible for any one who was not a prig to keep to the archaic attitude and parlance which the author attempts here and there; and I wish he had frankly refused to attempt it at all. I wish his personal recollections of Joan could have been written by some Southwestern American, translated to Domremy by some such mighty magic of imagination as launched the Connecticut Yankee into the streets of many-towered Camelot; but I make the most of the moments when the Sieur Louis de Conte forgets himself into much the sort of witness I could wish him to be. I am not at all troubled when he comes out with a bit of good, strong, downright modern American feeling; my suffering begins when he does the supposed mediæval thing. Then I suspect that his armor is of tin, that the castles and rocks are pasteboard, that the mob of citizens and soldiers who fill the air with the clash of their two-up-and-two-down combats, and the well-known muffled roar of their voices have been hired in at so much a night, and that Joan is sometimes in an awful temper behind the scenes; and I am thankful when the brave Sieur Louis forgets himself again. I have my little theory that human nature is elementally much the same always and everywhere, and that if the man of intelligence will study this in his own heart he will know pretty well what all other men have been in essentials. As to manners, I think that a man who knew the Southwest in the days of slavery, when the primitive distinctions between high and low, bond and free, lord and villein, were enforced with the violence of passions stronger than the laws, could make a shrewd guess at mediæval life; and I am inclined to accept Mark Twain's feudal ruffians, gentle and simple, as like enough, or as much like as one can get them at this late day. At least, they are like something, and the trouble with the more romantic reproductions is that they are like nothing.

A jolly thing about it, and a true thing, is the fun that his people get out of the affair. It is a vast frolic, in certain aspects, that mystical mission of the inspired Maid, and Joan herself is not above having her laugh at times. Her men-at-arms, who drive the English before them under her miraculous lead, are " the boys " who like to drink deep and to talk tall; to get the joke on one another, and the dead wood. Without this sort of relief I own that I should find their campaigns rather trying, and, without the hope of overhearing some of their lusty drollery, I should not care to follow them in all their hard fighting. I fancy it is the chance of this that gives the author himself so much stomach for battle; it seems worth while to lay a lot of fellows in plate-armor low if you can have them clatter down to the music of a burly jest and a roaring laugh. He is not at the trouble to maintain the solemnity of the dominant strain throughout; and he has made his Sieur de Conte not only a devout believer in the divine authority of Joan, but a delicately tender sympathizer with her when she suffers as a poor, simple shepherd-girl for the deeds of the prophetess. De Conte is a very human and lovable character, and is rather apt to speak with the generous feeling and the righteous love and hate of Mark Twain, whose humor has never been sullied with anything mean or cruel. The minor note is heard mostly through De Conte's story of the trial and martyrdom of Joan, which is studied faithfully from the histories, and which I think is the best part of the book. It is extremely pathetic at moments, and as one reads the heart swells with pity for the victim of one of the cruelest wrongs ever done, as if the suffering from it were not over four hundred years ago.

It would not be easy to convey a sense of the reverent tenderness with which the character of Joan is developed in this fiction, and she is made a " sensible, warm motion " from the myth that she seems in history. The wonder of her career is something that grows upon the reader to the end, and remains with him while he is left tingling with compassion for the hapless child who lived so gloriously and died so piteously.

What can we say, in this age of science, that will explain away the miracle of that age of faith? For these things really happened. There was actually this peasant maid who believed she heard voices from Heaven bidding her take command of the French armies and drive the English out of her country; who

took command of them without other authority than
such as the belief of her prince and his people gave
her; who prophesied of the victories she should win,
and won them; who broke the power of the invaders;
and who then, as if God thought she had given proofs
enough of her divine commission, fell into their power
and was burned for a heretic and an idolater. It reads
like a wild and foolish invention, but it is every word
most serious truth. It is preposterous, it is impossible,
but it is all undeniable.

What can we say to it in the last year of this incredulous old century, nodding to its close? We cannot deny it. What was it all? Was Joan's power the
force dormant in the people which her claim of inspiration awoke to mighty deeds? If it was merely
that, how came this poor, ignorant girl by the skill to
lead armies, to take towns, to advise councils, and to
change the fate of a whole nation? It was she who
recreated France, and changed her from a province of
England to the great monarchy she became. Could
a dream, an illusion, a superstition, do this? What,
then, are dreams and illusions and superstitions, that
our wisdom should be so eager to get rid of them?

We know that for the present the force which could
remove mountains is pretty much gone out of the world.
Faith has ceased to be, but we have some lively hopes
of electricity. We now employ it to exanimate people;
perhaps we shall yet find it valuable to reanimate them.
Or will faith come back again, and will the future ages
be some of them religious?

I shall not attempt to answer these questions, which
have, with a good number of others, been suggested by
this curious book of the arch-humorist of the century.
I fancy they will occur to most other readers, who will
share my interest in the devout, the mystical, the

knightly treatment of the story of Joan of Arc by
Mark Twain. Voltaire tried to make her a laughing-
stock and a by-word. He was a very great wit, but
he failed to defame her, for the facts were against him.
It is our humorist's fortune to have the facts with him,
and whatever we think Joan of Arc, inspired or de-
luded, we shall feel the wonder of them the more for
the light his imagination has thrown upon them. I
dare say there are a good many faults in the book. It
is unequal; its archaism is often superficially a failure; if you look at it merely on the technical side, the
outbursts of the nineteenth-century American in the
armor of the fifteenth-century Frenchman are sole-
cisms. But, in spite of all this, the book has a vital-
izing force. Joan lives in it again, and dies, and then
lives on in the love and pity and wonder of the reader.

X

REVIEW OF AN ITALIAN'S VIEWS OF MARK TWAIN[1]

(From " The North American Review," November, 1901)

Signor Bellezza talks, and we all talk, of English humor, American humor, German humor, Spanish humor, French humor, Italian humor, as if they were essentially unlike, when essentially they are alike. I will not try to say how, for that way danger lies: the danger of trying to say what humor essentially is. I notice Signor Bellezza himself shuns that as much as possible, and contents himself with giving instances without theories. We know a joke when we see it, as we know a poem when we see it; but what a joke is we can no more safely undertake to say than what a poem is. There the thing is: like it or leave it, but do not expect any one to explain to you the grounds of your liking or leaving it. That is what Signor Bellezza mainly seems to say, and he is quite in the right. If he sometimes tries to distinguish between the different kinds of humor, by nationalities, it is perhaps because he has been tempted beyond his strength. For my own part, in the kind of humor which I know

---

[1] Paolo Bellezza. *Humour.* Strenna a Beneficio del Pio Instituto dei Rachitici. 1900.

157

best—the American, namely—I have found examples
of it in regions so remote that I have been forced to
choose between faith in the solidarity of humor everywhere, and fear that the aliens are now and then able,
by means of some telepathic plagiary, to pilfer us of
our good things before we say them.

I was always amused by the saying of a Western
farmer in a very wet season that " It rained and rained,
and after awhile it got so it set up nights and rained."
But in Switzerland I heard of an old peasant who re-
marked of a very cold season, " The winter has come
to spend the summer with us," and then I felt that all
republican peoples were really one, or else that American humor and Swiss humor were of the same native
picturesqueness.

In that chapter on grisly humor, which is one of the
best in the book, and is the longest, we Americans enter
freely, and chiefly, as we should, in the person of Mark
Twain, who is cited four times to Thackeray's once,
though he is distanced by Dickens. It is interesting to
note how universal this humor is, and it seems to be
really the most humorous humor, in imparting that
shock of contrasts, which seems to be the essence of
humor, or its prime motive. Shakespeare, Fielding,
Guerrazzi, Godfrey Keller, Bret Harte, Heine, Que-
vedo, Addison, Larra, Kipling, Steele, Flaubert, Al-
fieri, Byron, Daudet, Dostoyevsky, Balzac, Hoffmann,
and Charles Mathews are by no means all the others
who figure in this famous chapter, in support of my
theory that humor is human and not national. When
it comes to grinning back at skeletons, mocking at
murder, and smiling at suicide it appears that Americans, Englishmen, Germans, Italians, Spaniards, and
Frenchmen are pretty much alike. The honors are not
quite so easy in the matter of gallows - humor; the

North carries these off, as has already been allowed.
In regard to cannibalism, Signor Bellezza thinks it the
forte of Mark Twain, as a humorous inspiration.
"And here," he says, "I do not mean fugitive
touches, but whole stories based, if I may so express
myself, upon anthropophagy," and in sufficient proof
he limits himself to a synopsis of that terrible tale of
Cannibalism in the Cars, which has made us all shud-
der. He seems not to know of that yet awfuler adventure with the box of rifles in the express-car, which
in the way of grisly humor may challenge all literature
for its like. In bizarre humor he puts us well toward
the head, instancing from Mark Twain a passage out of
Adam's Diary, registering Adam's speculations as to
the real nature of his first born and his place in zoology,
and *Lucretia Smith's Soldier,* whom Lucretia nurses
back to life and finds the wrong man when he is well
enough to have the bandages taken from his face. . . .

I am tempted to throw together what Signor Bellezza
has to say of most significance concerning all the aspects of the business in hand. He confesses: "If I
had to make a treatise in due form, or, rather, a regular
discourse, I should find myself baffled at the start, because all treatises commence, as is just, with a bold
definition, and humor cannot be defined. . . . It is a
specialty of the Northern peoples, somewhat like the
beer that we meridional folk find somewhat harsh to
the palate, and would not like for our daily drink. It
is neither acuteness, nor grace, nor *verve;* it has generally a serious aspect when all around are laughing,
as Addison says, . . . and according to the greatest
living humorist, Mark Twain, 'the humorist when he
tells a story seems not to have the remotest suspicion
that there is anything funny in it.' . . . Precisely here
is the essential difference that distinguishes the hu-

morous from the comic, of which it is yet a form; it
springs rather from a contrast, and the contrast is . . .
that of sorrow and joy, a pathetic situation and a comic
circumstance; as has been felicitously said, 'it is an
oscillation between laughter and tears.' . . . The humorist forbears the jeremiad, the lamentation, even
when his soul is running over with anguish. He would
not shed rivers of tears over the fate of man here below, doomed to yearn for the true, and to know it only
with sore labor and in little part; but he will content
himself in agreeing with Larra, that 'all the truths
in this world could be written on a cigarette paper.'
The social injustices that provoke the invectives of the
pessimist and the sociologist he will formulate in the
fashion of that famous sentence of Guerrazzi, 'Force is
the great mother Eve of all the rights.' . . . But here
let us understand ourselves clearly. If humor con-
sisted solely in recognizing and formulating the relations that connect joy and sorrow, their confusion and
their perennial alternation one after the other in human destiny, I should be ready to say that the humorists were as numerous as the authors—in fact, as men
themselves. . . . The humorist is he who does not keep
on singing this truth in all the various tunes, but is
intimately seized and pervaded by it, and informs his
thoughts and his works from it."

This is very well as far as it goes, but here nothing
can go to the bottom; for if it could, humor is so deeply
founded in human nature that any definition which
reached it would be in danger of coming out on the
other side, and proving a luminous concept of pathos.
Our author makes a better try in saying of the humorist, "He does not know how to remain long, or
will not, in a situation affecting, dramatic or otherwise
serious; but he interrupts it brusquely with some un-

expected observation that scatters, or, so to speak, disorients the ideas and sensations of the reader, and gives them a new direction." Again he says, beginning a fresh chapter, as he is apt to do with a fresh attempt at analysis: "Humor is truly among the literary kinds that which can be contained in the smallest terms. Nothing is too little; it finds its occasion in everything, even that which is slightest, thinnest, most impalpable, and for this reason it is difficult to analyze it. It lurks, let me say, in a parenthesis, in a comparison; the more modest the form it takes, the more vividly it frees itself and the more piquant it proves."

More than in any other literature, the humorous conception of the universe prevails in the English, and that is the supreme proof of humor. It is suggested in the passage which he quotes from Lucian, concerning that certain doubt of what shall be after death, which lurks in our laughter here, and mutes it on our trembling lips. It is this certain doubt which gives its prevailing cast to English literature more in the mother isle than in our continental condition of it; and it is literature which is the expression of a people's soul. To us belongs the humor that laughs and makes laugh; I believe Mark Twain himself somewhere claims that our humor is the only humor that is funny, and without pushing this claim we can allow that it is funnier than the English. It may even be as wise, and yet at the end of the ends it is not so satisfying; so that one agrees with Signor Bellezza's final judgment when he declares Mark Twain to be the greatest living humorist. . . . He is not only the greatest living humorist, but incomparably the greatest, and without a rival since Cervantes and Shakespeare, unless it be that eternal Jew, Heinrich Heine, who of all the humorists is the least

like him. Heine's humor is at every moment autobiographical, and for far the greater part Mr. Clemens's
humor is so; Shakespeare's alone is impersonal, but
this may be on account of the dramatic form, and more
apparent than real. Heine and Mark Twain are both
archromantic, just as they are both autobiographical,
though to what different ends! One is subjectively romantic and personal, the other objectively romantic and
personal. Mark Twain expresses in this difference the
very essence and inalienable intent of American humor,
which is apparently the least conscious and really the
least literary of all the forms and phases of humor,
while Heine's is the most conscious and the most literary. Is this measurably true of the other German
humorists? I am not sure, and I cannot pretend to
have the documents for the verification of the point.
Of Heine I can more or less honestly speak, but as
for the other German humorists, life is short, and art
in them at least seems very long. The most wonderful
thing in Heine is how he transmutes literature into
life, and distills into it the blood and tears of literary
anguish. Am I saying that he is a poseur? Perhaps
I am saying that, but while he lay there in his mattress-
grave in Paris, he mocked and mocked, not less than
in his books, or at least when he had an audience; and
no doubt the second nature which comes to men from
bathing their souls in literature had made itself his
first nature. He expressed the supreme humoristic conception of the universe in the cry from that grave:

"O schöne Welt, du bist abscheulich!"

and one's heart aches in pity and one's nerves thrill in
awe of the poseur. After all, pain is not a pose, nor
death, and there he knew both. In all his books he

was at least true to his genius, for, in some light or other, everything that he wrote was humorous. . . .

I doubt whether our humor did not begin with Chaucer instead of Shakespeare, and it is not at this end of the long line that I should find our essayist of an uncertain hold. It is in his notices of modern English humor that I find his hand lax, and now and then not of a wide grasp. He prefaces each of his chapters with an English motto, taking the first from Mark Twain's reply to M. Bourget, " Well, humor is the great thing," but by far the greatest number of his instances and allusions are from and to the humor of Dickens. Now, this humor was very well in its way, but it hardly can make us laugh any more, and it was always rather of the nature of the laughter of horses, the play of horses. It was fantastic and wilful and forced, and expressed itself in characters which bore much the same resemblance to the human species as the effigies which keep the crows from the corn-fields, and in crude communities express the popular indignation with persons of opposite political convictions. He had not a humorous conception of life, which is the great thing rather than humor itself, if Mark Twain, who has it, will allow me to dispute him. Dickens was a great histrionic talent, and produced powerful if simple effects in that sort. But he was not of the fine English humorists who began with Chaucer, or with Shakespeare, as you please, and came down with Swift, and Addison, and Steele, and Sterne, and Goldsmith, and perhaps Scott, and Thackeray, to a humorist who may almost stand with Shakespeare himself. I mean Mr. Thomas Hardy, who in his vision of humanity, in his entirely ironical and humorous conception of life, is possibly the greatest of all the present English, and I am not forgetting the Scotchman, Mr. William Gilbert,

I am remembering that the master of the whimsical
cannot be the equal of a humorist in whom the sense
of the droll is never parted from the sense of the dreadful, any more than it is in Heine, in whom the pathetic
prevails, or Mark Twain, in whom the comic prevails.

XI

MARK TWAIN: AN INQUIRY

(From " The North American Review," February, 1901)

Two recent events have concurred to offer criticism a fresh excuse, if not a fresh occasion, for examining the literary work of Mr. Samuel L. Clemens, better known to the human family by his pseudonym of Mark Twain. One of these events is the publication of his writings in a uniform edition, which it is to be hoped will remain indefinitely incomplete; the other is his return to his own country after an absence so long as to form a psychological perspective in which his characteristics make a new appeal.

The uniform edition of Mr. Clemens's writings is of that dignified presence which most of us have thought their due in moments of high pleasure with their quality, and high dudgeon with their keeping in the matchlessly ugly subscription volumes of the earlier issues. Yet now that we have them in this fine shape, fit every one, in its elect binding, paper, and print, to be set on the shelf of a gentleman's library, and not taken from it without some fear of personal demerit, I will own a furtive regret for the hideous blocks and bricks of which the visible temple of the humorist's fame was first builded. It was an advantage to meet the author in a guise reflecting the accidental and provisional moods of a unique talent finding itself out; and the pictures which originally illustrated the process were helps to the imagination such as the new uniform edition does not afford.   In great part it could not retain them, for reasons which the recollection of their uncouth vigor will suggest, but these reasons do not hold in all cases, and especially in the case of Mr. Dan Beard's extraordinarily sympathetic and interpretative pictures for *The Connecticut Yankee in King Arthur's Court*.   The illustrations of the uniform edition, in fact, are its weak side, but it can be said that they do not detract from one's delight in the literature; no illustrations could do that; and, in compensation for their defeat, the reader has the singularly intelligent and agreeable essay of Mr. Brander Matthews on Mr. Clemens's work by way of introduction to the collection. For the rest one may acquit one's self of one's whole duty to the uniform edition by reminding the reader that in the rich variety of its inclusion are those renowning books *The Innocents Abroad* and *Roughing It;* the first constructive fiction on the larger scale, *Tom Sawyer* and *Huckleberry Finn;* the later books of travel, *A Tramp Abroad* and *Following the Equator;* the multiplicity of tales, sketches, burlesques, satires, and speeches, together with the spoil of Mr. Clemens's courageous forays in the region of literary criticism; and his later romances, *The Connecticut Yankee, The American Claimant,* and *Joan of Arc*.   These complete an array of volumes which the most unconventional reviewer can hardly keep from calling goodly, and which is responsive to the spirit of the literature in a certain desultory and insuccessive arrangement.

So far as I know, Mr. Clemens is the first writer to use in extended writing the fashion we all use in think-

ing, and to set down the thing that comes into his
mind without fear or favor of the thing that went before or the thing that may be about to follow. I, for
instance, in putting this paper together, am anxious to
observe some sort of logical order, to discipline such
impressions and notions as I have of the subject into
a coherent body which shall march columnwise to a
conclusion obvious if not inevitable from the start.
But Mr. Clemens, if he were writing it, would not be
anxious to do any such thing. He would take whatever offered itself to his hand out of that mystical
chaos, that divine ragbag, which we call the mind,
and leave the reader to look after relevancies and sequences for himself. These there might be, but not
of that hard-and-fast sort which I am eager to lay
hold of, and the result would at least be satisfactory
to the author, who would have shifted the whole responsibility to the reader, with whom it belongs, at
least as much as with the author. In other words, Mr.
Clemens uses in work on the larger scale the method
of the elder essayists, and you know no more where you
are going to bring up in *The Innocents Abroad* or
Following the Equator than in an essay of Montaigne.
The end you arrive at is the end of the book, and you
reach it amused but edified, and sorry for nothing but
to be there. You have noted the author's thoughts,
but not his order of thinking; he has not attempted to
trace the threads of association between the things that
have followed one another; his reason, not his logic,
has convinced you, or, rather, it has persuaded you,
for you have not been brought under conviction. It is
not certain that this method is of design with Mr.
Clemens; that might spoil it; and possibly he will be
as much surprised as any one to know that it is his
method. It is imaginable that he pursues it from no

wish but to have pleasure of his work, and not to fatigue either himself or his reader; and his method may be the secret of his vast popularity, but it cannot be the whole secret of it. Any one may compose a scrap-book, and offer it to the public with nothing of Mark Twain's good-fortune. Everything seems to depend upon the nature of the scraps, after all; his scraps might have been consecutively arranged, in a studied order, and still have immensely pleased; but there is no doubt that people like things that have at least the appearance of not having been drilled into line. Life itself has that sort of appearance as it goes on; it is an essay with moments of drama in it rather than a drama; it is a lesson, with the precepts appearing hap-hazard, and not precept upon precept; it is a school, but not always a school-room; it is a temple, but the priests are not always in their sacerdotal robes; some-times they are eating the sacrifice behind the altar and pouring the libations for the god through the channels of their dusty old throats. An instinct of something chaotic, ironic, empiric in the order of experience seems to have been the inspiration of our humorist's art, and what finally remains with the reader, after all the jok-ing and laughing, is not merely the feeling of having had a mighty good time, but the conviction that he has got the worth of his money. He has not gone through the six hundred pages of *The Innocents Abroad*, or *Following the Equator,* without having learned more of the world as the writer saw it than any but the rarest traveller is able to show for his travel; and pos-sibly, with his average practical American public, which was his first tribunal, and must always be his court of final appeal, Mark Twain justified himself for being so delightful by being so instructive. If this bold notion is admissible, it seems the moment to say that no writer ever imparted information more inoffensively.

But his great charm is his absolute freedom in a region where most of us are fettered and shackled by immemorial convention. He saunters out into the trim world of letters, and lounges across its neatly kept paths, and walks about on the grass at will, in spite of all the signs that have been put up from the beginning of literature, warning people of dangers and penalties for the slightest trespass.

One of the characteristics I observe in him is his single-minded use of words, which he employs as Grant did to express the plain, straight meaning their common acceptance has given them with no regard to their structural significance or their philological implications. He writes English as if it were a primitive and not a derivative language, without Gothic or Latin or Greek behind it, or German and French beside it. The result is the English in which the most vital works of English literature are cast, rather than the English of Milton and Thackeray and Mr. Henry James. I do not say that the English of the authors last named is less than vital, but only that it is not the most vital. It is scholarly and conscious; it knows who its grandfather was; it has the refinement and subtlety of an old patriciate. You will not have with it the widest suggestion, the largest human feeling, or perhaps the loftiest reach of imagination, but you will have the keen joy that exquisite artistry in words can alone impart, and that you will not have in Mark Twain. What you will have in him is a style which is as personal, as biographical as the style of any one who has written, and expresses a civilization whose courage of the chances, the preferences, the duties, is not the measure of its essential modesty. It has a thing to say, and it says it in the word that may be the first or second or third choice, but will not be the instrument of the most fastidious ear, the most delicate and exacting sense, though it will be the word that surely and strongly conveys intention from the author's mind to the reader's. It is the Abraham Lincolnian word, not the Charles Sumnerian; it is American, Western.

Now that Mark Twain has become a fame so world-wide, we should be in some danger of forgetting, but for his help, how entirely American he is, and we have already forgotten, perhaps, how truly Western he is, though his work, from first to last, is always reminding us of the fact. But here I should like to distinguish. It is not alone in its generous humor, with more honest laughter in it than humor ever had in the world till now, that his work is so Western. Any one who has really known the West (and really to know it one must have lived it) is aware of the profoundly serious, the almost tragical strain which is the fundamental tone in the movement of such music as it has. Up to a certain point, in the presence of the mystery which we call life, it trusts and hopes and laughs; beyond that it doubts and fears, but it does not cry. It is more likely to laugh again, and in the work of Mark Twain there is little of the pathos which is supposed to be the ally of humor, little suffusion of apt tears from the smiling eyes. It is too sincere for that sort of play; and if after the doubting and the fearing it laughs again, it is with a suggestion of that resentment which youth feels when the disillusion from its trust and hope comes, and which is the grim second-mind of the West in the presence of the mystery. It is not so much the race-effect as the region-effect; it is not the Anglo-American finding expression, it is the Westerner, who is not more thoroughly the creature of cir-

cumstances, of conditions, but far more dramatically
their creature than any prior man. He found himself
placed in them and under them, so near to a world in
which the natural and primitive was obsolete, that
while he could not escape them, neither could he help
challenging them. The inventions, the appliances, the
improvements of the modern world invaded the hoary
eld of his rivers and forests and prairies, and, while he
was still a pioneer, a hunter, a trapper, he found himself confronted with the financier, the scholar, the
gentleman. They seemed to him, with the world they
represented, at first very droll, and he laughed. Then
they set him thinking, and, as he never was afraid of
anything, he thought over the whole field and demanded
explanations of all his prepossessions—of equality, of
humanity, of representative government, and revealed
religion. When they had not their answers ready,
without accepting the conventions of the modern world
as solutions or in any manner final, he laughed again,
not mockingly, but patiently, compassionately. Such,
or somewhat like this, was the genesis and evolution of
Mark Twain.

Missouri was Western, but it was also Southern, not
only in the institution of slavery, to the custom and acceptance of which Mark Twain was born and bred without any applied doubt of its divinity, but in the peculiar social civilization of the older South from which
his native State was settled. It would be reaching too
far out to claim that American humor, of the now prevailing Western type, is of Southern origin, but without staying to attempt it I will say that I think the
fact could be established; and I think one of the most
notably Southern traits of Mark Twain's humor is its
power of seeing the fun of Southern seriousness, but
this vision did not come to him till after his liberation

from neighborhood in the vaster Far West. He was the first, if not the only, man of his section to betray a consciousness of the grotesque absurdities in the Southern inversion of the civilized ideals in behalf of slavery, which must have them upside down in order to walk over them safely. No American of Northern birth or breeding could have imagined the spiritual struggle of Huck Finn in deciding to help the negro Jim to his freedom, even though he should be forever despised as a negro thief in his native town, and perhaps eternally lost through the blackness of his sin. No Northerner could have come so close to the heart of a Kentucky feud, and revealed it so perfectly, with the whimsicality playing through its carnage, or could have so brought us into the presence of the sardonic comi-tragedy of the squalid little river town where the store-keeping magnate shoots down his drunken tormentor in the arms of the drunkard's daughter, and then cows with bitter mockery the mob that comes to lynch him. The strict religiosity compatible in the Southwest with savage precepts of conduct is something that could make itself known in its amusing contrast only to the native Southwesterner, and the revolt against it is as constant in Mark Twain as the enmity to New England orthodoxy is in Doctor Holmes. But he does not take it with such serious resentment as Doctor Holmes is apt to take his inherited Puritanism, and it may be therefore that he is able to do it more perfect justice, and impart it more absolutely. At any rate, there are no more vital passages in his fiction than those which embody character as it is affected for good as well as evil by the severity of the local Sunday-schooling and church-going.

I find myself, in spite of the discipline I intend for this paper, speaking first of the fiction, which by no means came first in Mark Twain's literary development. It is true that his beginnings were in short sketches, more or less inventive, and studies of life in which he let his imagination play freely; but it was not till he had written *Tom Sawyer* that he could be called a novelist. Even now I think he should rather be called a romancer, though such a book as *Huckleberry Finn* takes itself out of the order of romance and places itself with the great things in picaresque fiction. Still, it is more poetic than picaresque, and of a deeper psychology. The probable and credible soul that the author divines in the son of the town-drunkard is one which we might each own brother, and the art which portrays this nature at first hand in the person and language of the hero, without pose or affectation, is fine art. In the boy's history the author's fancy works realistically to an end as high as it has reached elsewhere, if not higher; and I who like *The Connecticut Yankee in King Arthur's Court* so much have half a mind to give my whole heart to *Huckleberry Finn*.

Both *Huckleberry Finn* and *Tom Sawyer* wander in episodes loosely related to the main story, but they are of a closer and more logical advance from the beginning to the end than the fiction which preceded them, and which I had almost forgotten to name before them. We owe to *The Gilded Age* a type in Colonel Mulberry Sellers which is as likely to endure as any fictitious character of our time. It embodies the sort of Americanism which survived through the Civil War, and characterized in its boundlessly credulous, fearlessly adventurous, unconsciously burlesque excess the period of political and economic expansion which followed the war. Colonel Sellers was, in some rough sort, the American of that day, which already seems so remote, and is best imaginable through him. Yet the story itself was of the fortuitous structure of what may be called the autobiographical books, such as *The Innocents Abroad* and *Roughing It.* Its desultory and accidental character was heightened by the co-operation of Mr. Clemens's fellow-humorist, Charles Dudley Warner, and such coherence as it had was weakened by the diverse qualities of their minds and their irreconcilable ideals in literature. These never combined to a sole effect or to any variety of effects that left the reader very clear what the story was all about; and yet from the cloudy solution was precipitated at least one character which, as I have said, seems of as lasting substance and lasting significance as any which the American imagination has evolved from the American environment.

If Colonel Sellers is Mr. Clemens's supreme invention, as it seems to me, I think that his *Connecticut Yankee* is his highest achievement in the way of a greatly imagined and symmetrically developed romance. Of all the fanciful schemes in fiction, it pleases me most, and I give myself with absolute delight to its notion of a keen East Hartford Yankee finding himself, by a retroactionary spell, at the court of King Arthur of Britain, and becoming part of the sixth century with all the customs and ideas of the nineteenth in him and about him. The field for humanizing satire which this scheme opens is illimitable; but the ultimate achievement, the last poignant touch, the most exquisite triumph of the book, is the return of the Yankee to his own century, with his look across the gulf of the ages at the period of which he had been a part and his vision of the sixth-century woman he had loved holding their child in her arms.

It is a great fancy, transcending in æsthetic beauty the invention in *The Prince and the Pauper,* with all the delightful and affecting implications of that charming fable, and excelling the heartrending story in which Joan of Arc lives and prophesies and triumphs and suffers. She is, indeed, realized to the modern sense as few figures of the past have been realized in fiction; and is none the less of her time and of all time because her supposititious historian is so recurrently of ours. After Sellers, and Huck Finn, and Tom Sawyer, and the Connecticut Yankee, she is the author's finest creation; and if he had succeeded in portraying no other woman - nature, he would have approved himself its fit interpreter in her. I do not think he succeeds so often with that nature as with the boy-nature or the man - nature, apparently because it does not interest him so much. He will not trouble himself to make women talk like women at all times; oftentimes they talk too much like him, though the simple, homely sort express themselves after their kind; and Mark Twain does not always write men's dialogue so well as he might. He is apt to burlesque the lighter colloquiality, and it is only in the more serious and most tragical junctures that his people utter themselves with veracious simplicity and dignity. That great, burly fancy of his is always tempting him to the exaggeration which is the condition of so much of his personal humor, but which when it invades the drama spoils the illusion. The illusion renews itself in the great moments, but I wish it could be kept intact in the small, and I blame him that he does not rule his fancy better. His imagination is always dramatic in its conceptions, but not always in its expressions; the talk of his people is often inadequate caricature in the ordinary exigencies, and his art contents itself with makeshift in the minor action. Even in *Huck Finn,* so admirably proportioned and honestly studied, you find a piece of lawless extravagance hurled in, like the episode of the two strolling actors in the flatboat; their broad burlesque is redeemed by their final tragedy—a prodigiously real and moving passage—but the friend of the book cannot help wishing the burlesque was not there. One laughs, and then despises one's self for laughing, and this is not what Mark Twain often makes you do. There are things in him that shock, and more things that we think shocking, but this may not be so much because of their nature as because of our want of naturalness; they wound our conventions rather than our convictions. As most women are more the subjects of convention than men, his humor is not for most women; but I have a theory that, when women like it, they like it far beyond men. Its very excess must satisfy that demand of their insatiate nerves for something that there is enough of; but I offer this conjecture with instant readiness to withdraw it under correction. What I feel rather surer of is that there is something finally feminine in the inconsequence of his ratiocination, and his beautiful confidence that we shall be able to follow him to his conclusion in all those turnings and twistings and leaps and bounds by which his mind carries itself to any point but that he seems aiming at. Men, in fact, are born of women, and possibly Mark Twain owes his literary method to the colloquial style of some far ancestress who was more concerned in getting there, and amusing herself on the way, than in ordering her steps.

Possibly, also, it is to this ancestress that he owes the instinct of right and wrong which keeps him clear as to the conditions that formed him, and their injustice. Slavery in a small Missouri River town could not have been the dignified and patriarchal institution which Southerners of the older South are fond of remembering or imagining. In the second generation from Virginia ancestry of this sort, Mark Twain was born to the common necessity of looking out for himself, and, while making himself practically of another order of things, he felt whatever was fine in the old and could regard whatever was ugly and absurd more tolerantly, more humorously than those who bequeathed him their enmity to it. Fortunately for him, and for us who were to enjoy his humor, he came to his intellectual consciousness in a world so large and free and safe that he could be fair to any wrong while seeing the right so unfailingly; and nothing is finer in him than his gentleness with the error which is simply passive and negative. He gets fun out of it, of course, but he deals almost tenderly with it, and hoards his violence for the superstitions and traditions which are arrogant and active. His pictures of that old river-town, Southwestern life, with its faded and tattered aristocratic ideals and its squalid democratic realities, are pathetic, while they are so unsparingly true and so inapologetically and unaffectedly faithful.

The West, when it began to put itself into literature, could do so without the sense, or the apparent sense, of any older or politer world outside of it; whereas the East was always looking fearfully over its shoulder at Europe, and anxious to account for itself as well as represent itself. No such anxiety as this entered Mark Twain's mind, and it is not claiming too much for the Western influence upon American literature to say that the final liberation of the East from this anxiety is due to the West, and to its ignorant courage or its indifference to its difference from the rest of the world. It would not claim to be superior, as the South did, but it could claim to be humanly equal, or, rather, it would make no claim at all, but would simply be, and what it was, show itself without holding itself responsible for not being something else.

The Western boy of forty or fifty years ago grew up so close to the primeval woods or fields that their inarticulate poetry became part of his being, and he was apt to deal simply and uncritically with literature when he turned to it, as he dealt with nature. He took what he wanted, and left what he did not like; he used it for the playground, not the workshop of his spirit. Something like this I find true of Mark Twain in peculiar and uncommon measure. I do not see any proof in his books that he wished at any time to produce literature, or that he wished to reproduce life. When filled up with an experience that deeply interested him, or when provoked by some injustice or absurdity that intensely moved him, he burst forth, and the outbreak might be altogether humorous, but it was more likely to be humorous with a groundswell of seriousness carrying it profoundly forward. In all there is something curiously, not very definably, elemental, which again seems to me Western. He behaves himself as if he were the first man who was ever up against the proposition in hand. He deals as newly, for instance, with the relations of Shelley to his wife, and with as personal and direct an indignation, as if they had never attracted critical attention before; and this is the mind or the mood which he brings to all literature. Life is another affair with him; it is not a discovery, not a surprise; every one else knows how it is; but here is a new world, and he explores it with a ramping joy, and shouts for the reader to come on and see how, in spite of all the lies about it, it is the same old world of men and women, with really nothing in it but their passions and prejudices and hypocrisies. At heart he was always deeply and essentially romantic, and once must have expected life itself to be a fairy dream. When it did not turn out so he found it tremendously amusing still, and his expectation not the least amusing thing in it, but without rancor, without grudge or bitterness in his disillusion, so that his latest word is as sweet as his first. He is deeply and essentially romantic in his literary conceptions, but when it comes to working them out he is helplessly literal and real; he is the impassioned lover, the helpless slave of the concrete. For this reason, for his wish, his necessity, first to ascertain his facts, his logic is as irresistible as his laugh.

All life seems, when he began to find it out, to have the look of a vast joke, whether the joke was on him or on his fellow - beings, or if it may be expressed without irreverence, on their common creator. But it was never wholly a joke, and it was not long before his literature began to own its pathos. The sense of this is not very apparent in *The Innocents Abroad*, but in *Roughing It* we began to be distinctly aware of it, and in the successive books it is constantly imminent, not as a clutch at the heartstrings, but as a demand of common justice, common sense, the feeling of proportion. It is not sympathy with the under dog merely as under dog that moves Mark Twain; for the under dog is sometimes rightfully under. But the probability is that it is wrongfully under, and has a claim to your inquiry into the case which you cannot ignore without atrocity. Mark Twain never ignores it; I know nothing finer in him than his perception that in this curiously contrived mechanism men suffer for their sorrows rather oftener than they suffer for their sins; and when they suffer for their sorrows they have a right not only to our pity but to our help. He always gives his help, even when he seems to leave the pity to others, and it may be safely said that no writer has dealt with so many phases of life with more unfailing justice. There is no real telling how any one comes to be what he is; all speculation concerning the fact is more or less impudent or futile conjecture; but it is conceivable that Mark Twain took from his early environment the custom of clairvoyance in things in which most humorists are purblind, and that being always in the presence of the under dog, he came to feel for him as under with him. If the knowledge and vision of slavery did not tinge all life with potential tragedy, perhaps it was this which lighted in the future humorist the indignation at injustice which glows in his page. His indignation relieves itself as often as not in a laugh; injustice is the most ridiculous thing in the world, after all, and indignation with it feels its own absurdity.

It is supposable, if not more than supposable, that the ludicrous incongruity of a slaveholding democracy nurtured upon the Declaration of Independence, and the comical spectacle of white labor owning black labor, had something to do in quickening the sense of contrast which is the fountain of humor, or is said to be so. But not to drive too hard a conjecture which must remain conjecture, we may reasonably hope to find in the untrammelled, the almost unconditional life of the later and farther West, with its individualism limited by nothing but individualism, the outside causes of the first overflow of the spring. We are so fond of classification, which we think is somehow interpretation, that one cannot resist the temptation it holds out in the case of the most unclassifiable things; and I must yield so far as to note that the earliest form of Mark Twain's work is characteristic of the greater part of it. The method used in *The Innocents Abroad* and in

Roughing It is the method used in *Life on the Missis-sippi,* in *A Tramp Abroad,* and in *Following the Equator,* which constitute in bulk a good half of all his writings, as they express his dominant æsthetics. If he had written the fictions alone, we should have had to recognize a rare inventive talent, a great imagination and dramatic force; but I think it must be allowed that the personal books named overshadow the fictions. They have the qualities that give character to the fictions, and they have advantages that the fictions have not and that no fiction can have. In them, under cover of his pseudonym, we come directly into the presence of the author, which is what the reader is always longing and seeking to do; but unless the novelist is a conscienceless and tasteless recreant to the terms of his art, he cannot admit the reader to his intimacy. The personal books of Mark Twain have not only the charm of the essay's inconsequent and desultory method, in which invention, fact, reflection, and philosophy wander after one another in any following that happens, but they are of an immediate and most informal hospitality which admits you at once to the author's confidence, and makes you frankly welcome not only to his thought but to his way of thinking. He takes no trouble in the matter, and he asks you to take none. All that he requires is that you will have common sense, and be able to tell a joke when you see it. Otherwise the whole furnishing of his mental mansion is at your service, to make such use as you can of it, but he will not be always directing your course, or requiring you to enjoy yourself in this or that order.

In the case of the fictions, he conceives that his first affair is to tell a story, and a story when you are once launched upon it does not admit of deviation without some hurt to itself. In Mark Twain's novels, whether

they are for boys or for men, the episodes are only
those that illustrate the main narrative or relate to it,
though he might have allowed himself somewhat larger
latitude in the old-fashioned tradition which he has
oftenest observed in them. When it comes to the critical writings, which again are personal, and which,
whether they are criticisms of literature or of life, are
always so striking, he is quite relentlessly logical and
coherent. Here there is no lounging or sauntering,
with entertaining or edifying digressions. The object
is in view from the first, and the reasoning is straight-
forwardly to it throughout. This is as notable in the
admirable paper on the Jews, or on the Austrian situation, as in that on Harriet Shelley, or that on Cooper's
novels. The facts are first ascertained with a conscience uncommon in critical writing of any kind, and
then they are handled with vigor and precision till the
polemic is over. It does not so much matter whether
you agree with the critic or not; what you have to own
is that here is a man of strong convictions, clear ideas,
and ardent sentiments, based mainly upon common
sense of extraordinary depth and breadth.

In fact, what finally appeals to you in Mark Twain,
and what may hereafter be his peril with his readers,
is his common sense. It is well to eat humble pie when
one comes to it at the table d'hôte of life, and I wish
here to offer my brother literary men a piece of it that
I never refuse myself. It is true that other men do
not really expect much common sense of us, whether
we are poets or novelists or humorists. They may
enjoy our company, and they may like us or pity us,
but they do not take us very seriously, and they would
as soon we were fools as not if we will only divert or
comfort or inspire them. Especially if we are humorists do they doubt our practical wisdom; they are

apt at first sight to take our sense for a part of the joke, and the humorist who convinces them that he is a man of as much sense as any of them, and possibly more, is in the parlous case of having given them hostages for seriousness which he may not finally be able to redeem.

I should say in the haste to which every inquiry of this sort seems subject, that this was precisely the case with Mark Twain. The exceptional observer must have known from the beginning that he was a thinker of courageous originality and penetrating sagacity, even when he seemed to be joking; but in the process of time it has come to such a pass with him that the wayfaring man can hardly shirk knowledge of the fact. The fact is thrown into sudden and picturesque relief by his return to his country after the lapse of time long enough to have let a new generation grow up in knowledge of him. The projection of his reputation against a background of foreign appreciation, more or less luminous, such as no other American author has enjoyed, has little or nothing to do with his acceptance on the new terms. Those poor Germans, Austrians, Englishmen, and Frenchmen who have been, from time to time in the last ten years, trying to show their esteem for his peculiar gifts could never come as close to the heart of his humor as we could; we might well doubt if they could fathom all his wisdom, which begins and ends in his humor; and if ever they seemed to chance upon his full significance, we naturally felt a kind of grudge, when we could not call it their luck, and suspected him of being less significant in the given instances than they supposed. The danger which he now runs with us is neither heightened nor lessened by the spread of his fame, but is an effect from intrinsic causes. Possibly it might not have been so great if he had come back comparatively forgotten; it is certain only that in coming back more remembered than ever, he confronts a generation which began to know him not merely by his personal books and his fiction, but by those criticisms of life and literature which have more recently attested his interest in the graver and weightier things.

Graver and weightier, people call them, but whether they are really more important than the lighter things, I am by no means sure. What I am amused with, independently of the final truth, is the possibility that his newer audience will exact this serious mood of Mr. Clemens, whereas we of his older world only suffered it, and were of a high conceit with our liberality in allowing a humorist sometimes to be a philosopher. Some of us indeed, not to be invidiously specific as to whom, were always aware of potentialities in him, which he seemed to hold in check, or to trust doubtfully to his reader as if he thought they might be thought part of the joke. Looking back over his work now, the later reader would probably be able to point out to earlier readers the evidence of a constant growth in the direction of something like recognized authority in matters of public import, especially those that were subject to the action of the public conscience as well as the public interest, until now hardly any man writing upon such matters is heard so willingly by all sorts of men. All of us, for instance, have read somewhat of the conditions in South Africa which have eventuated in the present effort of certain British politicians to destroy two free republics in the interest of certain British speculators; but I doubt if we have found the case anywhere so well stated as in the closing chapters of Mark Twain's *Following the Equator*. His estimate of the military character of the belligerents on either side is of the prophetic cast which can come only from the thorough assimilation of accomplished facts; and in those passages the student of the actual war can spell its anticipative history. It is by such handling of such questions, unpremeditated and almost casual as it seems, that Mark Twain has won his claim to be heard on any public matter, and achieved the odd sort of primacy which he now enjoys.

But it would be rather awful if the general recognition of his prophetic function should implicate the renunciation of the humor that has endeared him to mankind. It would be well for his younger following to beware of reversing the error of the elder, and taking everything in earnest, as these once took nothing in earnest from him. To reverse that error would not be always to find his true meaning, and perhaps we shall best arrive at this by shunning one another's mistakes. In the light of the more modern appreciation, we elders may be able to see some things seriously that we once thought pure drolling, and from our experience his younger admirers may learn to receive as drolling some things that they might otherwise accept as preaching. What we all should wish to do is to keep Mark Twain what he has always been: a comic force unique in the power of charming us out of our cares and troubles, united with as potent an ethic sense of the duties, public and private, which no man denies in himself without being false to other men. I think we may hope for the best he can do to help us deserve our self-respect, without forming Mark Twain societies to read philanthropic meanings into his jokes, or studying the Jumping Frog as the allegory of an imperializing republic. I trust the time may be far distant when the Meditation at the Tomb of Adam shall be memorized and declaimed by ingenuous youth as a mystical appeal for human solidarity.

XII

THE AMERICAN JOKE

*(Read at the Birthday Dinner to S. L. Clemens,
December 5, 1905)*

I

A traveller from the Old World, just escaped
  Our Customs with his life, had found his way
To a place up-town, where a Colossus shaped
  Itself, sky-scraper high, against the day.
A vast smile, dawning from its mighty lips,
  Like sunshine on its visage seemed to brood;
One eye winked in perpetual eclipse,
  In the other a huge tear of pity stood.
Wisdom in nuggets round its temples shone;
  Its measureless bulk grotesque, exultant, rose;
And while Titanic puissance clothed it on,
  Patience with foreigners was in its pose.
So that, " What art thou?" the emboldened traveller
      spoke,
And it replied, " I am the American Joke.

II

" I am the joke that laughs the proud to scorn;
  I mock at cruelty, I banish care,
I cheer the lowly, chipper the forlorn,
  I bid the oppressor and hypocrite beware.

MY MARK TWAIN

I tell the tale that makes men cry for joy;
  I bring the laugh that has no hate in it;
In the heart of age I wake the undying boy;
  My big stick blossoms with a thornless wit,
The lame dance with delight in me; my mirth
  Reaches the deaf untrumpeted; the blind
My point can see. I jolly the whole earth,
  But most I love to jolly my own kind,
Joke of a people great, gay, bold, and free,
I type their master-mood. *Mark Twain made me.*"

                              W. D. HOWELLS.

THE END

A CATALOG OF SELECTED
DOVER BOOKS
IN ALL FIELDS OF INTEREST

A CATALOG OF SELECTED DOVER
BOOKS IN ALL FIELDS OF INTEREST

CONCERNING THE SPIRITUAL IN ART, Wassily Kandinsky. Pioneering work by father of abstract art. Thoughts on color theory, nature of art. Analysis of earlier masters. 12 illustrations. 80pp. of text. 5⅜ × 8½.   23411-8 Pa. $3.95

ANIMALS: 1,419 Copyright-Free Illustrations of Mammals, Birds, Fish, Insects, etc., Jim Harter (ed.). Clear wood engravings present, in extremely lifelike poses, over 1,000 species of animals. One of the most extensive pictorial sourcebooks of its kind. Captions. Index. 284pp. 9 × 12.   23766-4 Pa. $12.95

CELTIC ART: The Methods of Construction, George Bain. Simple geometric techniques for making Celtic interlacements, spirals, Kells-type initials, animals, humans, etc. Over 500 illustrations. 160pp. 9 × 12. (USO)   22923-8 Pa. $9.95

AN ATLAS OF ANATOMY FOR ARTISTS, Fritz Schider. Most thorough reference work on art anatomy in the world. Hundreds of illustrations, including selections from works by Vesalius, Leonardo, Goya, Ingres, Michelangelo, others. 593 illustrations. 192pp. 7⅛ × 10¼.   20241-0 Pa. $9.95

CELTIC HAND STROKE-BY-STROKE (Irish Half-Uncial from "The Book of Kells"): An Arthur Baker Calligraphy Manual, Arthur Baker. Complete guide to creating each letter of the alphabet in distinctive Celtic manner. Covers hand position, strokes, pens, inks, paper, more. Illustrated. 48pp. 8¼ × 11.
          24336-2 Pa. $3.95

EASY ORIGAMI, John Montroll. Charming collection of 32 projects (hat, cup, pelican, piano, swan, many more) specially designed for the novice origami hobbyist. Clearly illustrated easy-to-follow instructions insure that even beginning papercrafters will achieve successful results. 48pp. 8¼ × 11.   27298-2 Pa. $2.95

THE COMPLETE BOOK OF BIRDHOUSE CONSTRUCTION FOR WOOD-WORKERS, Scott D. Campbell. Detailed instructions, illustrations, tables. Also data on bird habitat and instinct patterns. Bibliography. 3 tables. 63 illustrations in 15 figures. 48pp. 5¼ × 8½.   24407-5 Pa. $1.95

BLOOMINGDALE'S ILLUSTRATED 1886 CATALOG: Fashions, Dry Goods and Housewares, Bloomingdale Brothers. Famed merchants' extremely rare catalog depicting about 1,700 products: clothing, housewares, firearms, dry goods, jewelry, more. Invaluable for dating, identifying vintage items. Also, copyright-free graphics for artists, designers. Co-published with Henry Ford Museum & Greenfield Village. 160pp. 8¼ × 11.   25780-0 Pa. $9.95

HISTORIC COSTUME IN PICTURES, Braun & Schneider. Over 1,450 costumed figures in clearly detailed engravings—from dawn of civilization to end of 19th century. Captions. Many folk costumes. 256pp. 8⅜ × 11¾.   23150-X Pa. $11.95

STICKLEY CRAFTSMAN FURNITURE CATALOGS, Gustav Stickley and L. & J. G. Stickley. Beautiful, functional furniture in two authentic catalogs from 1910. 594 illustrations, including 277 photos, show settles, rockers, armchairs, reclining chairs, bookcases, desks, tables. 183pp. 6½ × 9¼. 23838-5 Pa. $9.95

AMERICAN LOCOMOTIVES IN HISTORIC PHOTOGRAPHS: 1858 to 1949, Ron Ziel (ed.). A rare collection of 126 meticulously detailed official photographs, called "builder portraits," of American locomotives that majestically chronicle the rise of steam locomotive power in America. Introduction. Detailed captions. xi + 129pp. 9 × 12. 27393-8 Pa. $12.95

AMERICA'S LIGHTHOUSES: An Illustrated History, Francis Ross Holland, Jr. Delightfully written, profusely illustrated fact-filled survey of over 200 American lighthouses since 1716. History, anecdotes, technological advances, more. 240pp. 8 × 10¾. 25576-X Pa. $11.95

TOWARDS A NEW ARCHITECTURE, Le Corbusier. Pioneering manifesto by founder of "International School." Technical and aesthetic theories, views of industry, economics, relation of form to function, "mass-production split" and much more. Profusely illustrated. 320pp. 6⅛ × 9¼. (USO) 25023-7 Pa. $9.95

HOW THE OTHER HALF LIVES, Jacob Riis. Famous journalistic record, exposing poverty and degradation of New York slums around 1900, by major social reformer. 100 striking and influential photographs. 233pp. 10 × 7⅞.
22012-5 Pa $10.95

FRUIT KEY AND TWIG KEY TO TREES AND SHRUBS, William M. Harlow. One of the handiest and most widely used identification aids. Fruit key covers 120 deciduous and evergreen species; twig key 160 deciduous species. Easily used. Over 300 photographs. 126pp. 5⅜ × 8½. 20511-8 Pa. $3.95

COMMON BIRD SONGS, Dr. Donald J. Borror. Songs of 60 most common U.S. birds: robins, sparrows, cardinals, bluejays, finches, more—arranged in order of increasing complexity. Up to 9 variations of songs of each species.
Cassette and manual 99911-4 $8.95

ORCHIDS AS HOUSE PLANTS, Rebecca Tyson Northen. Grow cattleyas and many other kinds of orchids—in a window, in a case, or under artificial light. 63 illustrations. 148pp. 5⅜ × 8½. 23261-1 Pa. $4.95

MONSTER MAZES, Dave Phillips. Masterful mazes at four levels of difficulty. Avoid deadly perils and evil creatures to find magical treasures. Solutions for all 32 exciting illustrated puzzles. 48pp. 8¼ × 11. 26005-4 Pa. $2.95

MOZART'S DON GIOVANNI (DOVER OPERA LIBRETTO SERIES), Wolfgang Amadeus Mozart. Introduced and translated by Ellen H. Bleiler. Standard Italian libretto, with complete English translation. Convenient and thoroughly portable—an ideal companion for reading along with a recording or the performance itself. Introduction. List of characters. Plot summary. 121pp. 5¼ × 8½.
24944-1 Pa. $2.95

TECHNICAL MANUAL AND DICTIONARY OF CLASSICAL BALLET, Gail Grant. Defines, explains, comments on steps, movements, poses and concepts. 15-page pictorial section. Basic book for student, viewer. 127pp. 5⅜ × 8½.
21843-0 Pa. $4.95

BRASS INSTRUMENTS: Their History and Development, Anthony Baines. Authoritative, updated survey of the evolution of trumpets, trombones, bugles, cornets, French horns, tubas and other brass wind instruments. Over 140 illustrations and 48 music examples. Corrected and updated by author. New preface. Bibliography. 320pp. 5⅜ × 8½. 27574-4 Pa. $9.95

HOLLYWOOD GLAMOR PORTRAITS, John Kobal (ed.). 145 photos from 1926–49. Harlow, Gable, Bogart, Bacall; 94 stars in all. Full background on photographers, technical aspects. 160pp. 8⅜ × 11¼. 23352-9 Pa. $11.95

MAX AND MORITZ, Wilhelm Busch. Great humor classic in both German and English. Also 10 other works: "Cat and Mouse," "Plisch and Plumm," etc. 216pp. 5⅜ × 8½. 20181-3 Pa. $5.95

THE RAVEN AND OTHER FAVORITE POEMS, Edgar Allan Poe. Over 40 of the author's most memorable poems: "The Bells," "Ulalume," "Israfel," "To Helen," "The Conqueror Worm," "Eldorado," "Annabel Lee," many more. Alphabetic lists of titles and first lines. 64pp. 5³⁄₁₆ × 8¼. 26685-0 Pa. $1.00

SEVEN SCIENCE FICTION NOVELS, H. G. Wells. The standard collection of the great novels. Complete, unabridged. First Men in the Moon, Island of Dr. Moreau, War of the Worlds, Food of the Gods, Invisible Man, Time Machine, In the Days of the Comet. Total of 1,015pp. 5⅜ × 8½. (USO) 20264-X Clothbd. $29.95

AMULETS AND SUPERSTITIONS, E. A. Wallis Budge. Comprehensive discourse on origin, powers of amulets in many ancient cultures: Arab, Persian, Babylonian, Assyrian, Egyptian, Gnostic, Hebrew, Phoenician, Syriac, etc. Covers cross, swastika, crucifix, seals, rings, stones, etc. 584pp. 5⅜ × 8½. 23573-4 Pa. $12.95

RUSSIAN STORIES/PYCCKNE PACCKA3bl: A Dual-Language Book, edited by Gleb Struve. Twelve tales by such masters as Chekhov, Tolstoy, Dostoevsky, Pushkin, others. Excellent word-for-word English translations on facing pages, plus teaching and study aids, Russian/English vocabulary, biographical/critical introductions, more. 416pp. 5⅜ × 8½. 26244-8 Pa. $8.95

PHILADELPHIA THEN AND NOW: 60 Sites Photographed in the Past and Present, Kenneth Finkel and Susan Oyama. Rare photographs of City Hall, Logan Square, Independence Hall, Betsy Ross House, other landmarks juxtaposed with contemporary views. Captures changing face of historic city. Introduction. Captions. 128pp. 8¼ × 11. 25790-8 Pa. $9.95

AIA ARCHITECTURAL GUIDE TO NASSAU AND SUFFOLK COUNTIES, LONG ISLAND, The American Institute of Architects, Long Island Chapter, and the Society for the Preservation of Long Island Antiquities. Comprehensive, well-researched and generously illustrated volume brings to life over three centuries of Long Island's great architectural heritage. More than 240 photographs with authoritative, extensively detailed captions. 176pp. 8¼ × 11. 26946-9 Pa. $14.95

NORTH AMERICAN INDIAN LIFE: Customs and Traditions of 23 Tribes, Elsie Clews Parsons (ed.). 27 fictionalized essays by noted anthropologists examine religion, customs, government, additional facets of life among the Winnebago, Crow, Zuni, Eskimo, other tribes. 480pp. 6⅛ × 9¼. 27377-6 Pa. $10.95

FRANK LLOYD WRIGHT'S HOLLYHOCK HOUSE, Donald Hoffmann. Lavishly illustrated, carefully documented study of one of Wright's most controversial residential designs. Over 120 photographs, floor plans, elevations, etc. Detailed perceptive text by noted Wright scholar. Index. 128pp. 9¼ × 10¾.
27133-1 Pa. $11.95

THE MALE AND FEMALE FIGURE IN MOTION: 60 Classic Photographic Sequences, Eadweard Muybridge. 60 true-action photographs of men and women walking, running, climbing, bending, turning, etc., reproduced from rare 19th-century masterpiece. vi + 121pp. 9 × 12. 24745-7 Pa. $10.95

1001 QUESTIONS ANSWERED ABOUT THE SEASHORE, N. J. Berrill and Jacquelyn Berrill. Queries answered about dolphins, sea snails, sponges, starfish, fishes, shore birds, many others. Covers appearance, breeding, growth, feeding, much more. 305pp. 5¼ × 8¼. 23366-9 Pa. $7.95

GUIDE TO OWL WATCHING IN NORTH AMERICA, Donald S. Heintzelman. Superb guide offers complete data and descriptions of 19 species: barn owl, screech owl, snowy owl, many more. Expert coverage of owl-watching equipment, conservation, migrations and invasions, etc. Guide to observing sites. 84 illustrations. xiii + 193pp. 5⅜ × 8½. 27344-X Pa. $8.95

MEDICINAL AND OTHER USES OF NORTH AMERICAN PLANTS: A Historical Survey with Special Reference to the Eastern Indian Tribes, Charlotte Erichsen-Brown. Chronological historical citations document 500 years of usage of plants, trees, shrubs native to eastern Canada, northeastern U.S. Also complete identifying information. 343 illustrations. 544pp. 6½ × 9¼. 25951-X Pa. $12.95

STORYBOOK MAZES, Dave Phillips. 23 stories and mazes on two-page spreads: Wizard of Oz, Treasure Island, Robin Hood, etc. Solutions. 64pp. 8¼ × 11.
23628-5 Pa. $2.95

NEGRO FOLK MUSIC, U.S.A., Harold Courlander. Noted folklorist's scholarly yet readable analysis of rich and varied musical tradition. Includes authentic versions of over 40 folk songs. Valuable bibliography and discography. xi + 324pp. 5⅜ × 8½. 27350-4 Pa. $7.95

MOVIE-STAR PORTRAITS OF THE FORTIES, John Kobal (ed.). 163 glamor, studio photos of 106 stars of the 1940s: Rita Hayworth, Ava Gardner, Marlon Brando, Clark Gable, many more. 176pp. 8⅜ × 11¼. 23546-7 Pa. $11.95

BENCHLEY LOST AND FOUND, Robert Benchley. Finest humor from early 30s, about pet peeves, child psychologists, post office and others. Mostly unavailable elsewhere. 73 illustrations by Peter Arno and others. 183pp. 5⅜ × 8½.
22410-4 Pa. $5.95

YEKL and THE IMPORTED BRIDEGROOM AND OTHER STORIES OF YIDDISH NEW YORK, Abraham Cahan. Film Hester Street based on Yekl (1896). Novel, other stories among first about Jewish immigrants on N.Y.'s East Side. 240pp. 5⅜ × 8½. 22427-9 Pa. $6.95

SELECTED POEMS, Walt Whitman. Generous sampling from *Leaves of Grass*. Twenty-four poems include "I Hear America Singing," "Song of the Open Road," "I Sing the Body Electric," "When Lilacs Last in the Dooryard Bloom'd," "O Captain! My Captain!"—all reprinted from an authoritative edition. Lists of titles and first lines. 128pp. 5$\frac{3}{16}$ × 8¼. 26878-0 Pa. $1.00

THE BEST TALES OF HOFFMANN, E. T. A. Hoffmann. 10 of Hoffmann's most important stories: "Nutcracker and the King of Mice," "The Golden Flowerpot," etc. 458pp. 5⅜ × 8½. 21793-0 Pa. $8.95

FROM FETISH TO GOD IN ANCIENT EGYPT, E. A. Wallis Budge. Rich detailed survey of Egyptian conception of "God" and gods, magic, cult of animals, Osiris, more. Also, superb English translations of hymns and legends. 240 illustrations. 545pp. 5⅜ × 8½. 25803-3 Pa. $11.95

FRENCH STORIES/CONTES FRANÇAIS: A Dual-Language Book, Wallace Fowlie. Ten stories by French masters, Voltaire to Camus: "Micromegas" by Voltaire; "The Atheist's Mass" by Balzac; "Minuet" by de Maupassant; "The Guest" by Camus, six more. Excellent English translations on facing pages. Also French-English vocabulary list, exercises, more. 352pp. 5⅜ × 8½. 26443-2 Pa. $8.95

CHICAGO AT THE TURN OF THE CENTURY IN PHOTOGRAPHS: 122 Historic Views from the Collections of the Chicago Historical Society, Larry A. Viskochil. Rare large-format prints offer detailed views of City Hall, State Street, the Loop, Hull House, Union Station, many other landmarks, circa 1904–1913. Introduction. Captions. Maps. 144pp. 9⅜ × 12¼. 24656-6 Pa. $12.95

OLD BROOKLYN IN EARLY PHOTOGRAPHS, 1865–1929, William Lee Younger. Luna Park, Gravesend race track, construction of Grand Army Plaza, moving of Hotel Brighton, etc. 157 previously unpublished photographs. 165pp. 8⅞ × 11¾. 23587-4 Pa. $13.95

THE MYTHS OF THE NORTH AMERICAN INDIANS, Lewis Spence. Rich anthology of the myths and legends of the Algonquins, Iroquois, Pawnees and Sioux, prefaced by an extensive historical and ethnological commentary. 36 illustrations. 480pp. 5⅜ × 8½. 25967-6 Pa. $8.95

AN ENCYCLOPEDIA OF BATTLES: Accounts of Over 1,560 Battles from 1479 B.C. to the Present, David Eggenberger. Essential details of every major battle in recorded history from the first battle of Megiddo in 1479 B.C. to Grenada in 1984. List of Battle Maps. New Appendix covering the years 1967–1984. Index. 99 illustrations. 544pp. 6½ × 9¼. 24913-1 Pa. $14.95

SAILING ALONE AROUND THE WORLD, Captain Joshua Slocum. First man to sail around the world, alone, in small boat. One of great feats of seamanship told in delightful manner. 67 illustrations. 294pp. 5⅜ × 8½. 20326-3 Pa. $5.95

ANARCHISM AND OTHER ESSAYS, Emma Goldman. Powerful, penetrating, prophetic essays on direct action, role of minorities, prison reform, puritan hypocrisy, violence, etc. 271pp. 5⅜ × 8½. 22484-8 Pa. $5.95

MYTHS OF THE HINDUS AND BUDDHISTS, Ananda K. Coomaraswamy and Sister Nivedita. Great stories of the epics; deeds of Krishna, Shiva, taken from puranas, Vedas, folk tales; etc. 32 illustrations. 400pp. 5⅜ × 8½. 21759-0 Pa. $9.95

BEYOND PSYCHOLOGY, Otto Rank. Fear of death, desire of immortality, nature of sexuality, social organization, creativity, according to Rankian system. 291pp. 5⅜ × 8½. 20485-5 Pa. $8.95

A THEOLOGICO-POLITICAL TREATISE, Benedict Spinoza. Also contains unfinished Political Treatise. Great classic on religious liberty, theory of government on common consent. R. Elwes translation. Total of 421pp. 5⅜ × 8½. 20249-6 Pa. $8.95

MY BONDAGE AND MY FREEDOM, Frederick Douglass. Born a slave, Douglass became outspoken force in antislavery movement. The best of Douglass' autobiographies. Graphic description of slave life. 464pp. 5⅜ × 8½.   22457-0 Pa. $8.95

FOLLOWING THE EQUATOR: A Journey Around the World, Mark Twain. Fascinating humorous account of 1897 voyage to Hawaii, Australia, India, New Zealand, etc. Ironic, bemused reports on peoples, customs, climate, flora and fauna, politics, much more. 197 illustrations. 720pp. 5⅜ × 8½.   26113-1 Pa. $15.95

THE PEOPLE CALLED SHAKERS, Edward D. Andrews. Definitive study of Shakers: origins, beliefs, practices, dances, social organization, furniture and crafts, etc. 33 illustrations. 351pp. 5⅜ × 8½.   21081-2 Pa. $8.95

THE MYTHS OF GREECE AND ROME, H. A. Guerber. A classic of mythology, generously illustrated, long prized for its simple, graphic, accurate retelling of the principal myths of Greece and Rome, and for its commentary on their origins and significance. With 64 illustrations by Michelangelo, Raphael, Titian, Rubens, Canova, Bernini and others. 480pp. 5⅜ × 8½.   27584-1 Pa. $9.95

PSYCHOLOGY OF MUSIC, Carl E. Seashore. Classic work discusses music as a medium from psychological viewpoint. Clear treatment of physical acoustics, auditory apparatus, sound perception, development of musical skills, nature of musical feeling, host of other topics. 88 figures. 408pp. 5⅜ × 8½. 21851-1 Pa. $9.95

THE PHILOSOPHY OF HISTORY, Georg W. Hegel. Great classic of Western thought develops concept that history is not chance but rational process, the evolution of freedom. 457pp. 5⅜ × 8½.   20112-0 Pa. $9.95

THE BOOK OF TEA, Kakuzo Okakura. Minor classic of the Orient: entertaining, charming explanation, interpretation of traditional Japanese culture in terms of tea ceremony. 94pp. 5⅜ × 8½.   20070-1 Pa. $3.95

LIFE IN ANCIENT EGYPT, Adolf Erman. Fullest, most thorough, detailed older account with much not in more recent books, domestic life, religion, magic, medicine, commerce, much more. Many illustrations reproduce tomb paintings, carvings, hieroglyphs, etc. 597pp. 5⅜ × 8½.   22632-8 Pa. $10.95

SUNDIALS, Their Theory and Construction, Albert Waugh. Far and away the best, most thorough coverage of ideas, mathematics concerned, types, construction, adjusting anywhere. Simple, nontechnical treatment allows even children to build several of these dials. Over 100 illustrations. 230pp. 5⅜ × 8½.   22947-5 Pa. $7.95

DYNAMICS OF FLUIDS IN POROUS MEDIA, Jacob Bear. For advanced students of ground water hydrology, soil mechanics and physics, drainage and irrigation engineering, and more. 335 illustrations. Exercises, with answers. 784pp. 6⅛ × 9¼.   65675-6 Pa. $19.95

SONGS OF EXPERIENCE: Facsimile Reproduction with 26 Plates in Full Color, William Blake. 26 full-color plates from a rare 1826 edition. Includes "The Tyger," "London," "Holy Thursday," and other poems. Printed text of poems. 48pp. 5¼ × 7.   24636-1 Pa. $4.95

OLD-TIME VIGNETTES IN FULL COLOR, Carol Belanger Grafton (ed.). Over 390 charming, often sentimental illustrations, selected from archives of Victorian graphics—pretty women posing, children playing, food, flowers, kittens and puppies, smiling cherubs, birds and butterflies, much more. All copyright-free. 48pp. 9¼ × 12¼.   27269-9 Pa. $5.95

PERSPECTIVE FOR ARTISTS, Rex Vicat Cole. Depth, perspective of sky and sea, shadows, much more, not usually covered. 391 diagrams, 81 reproductions of drawings and paintings. 279pp. 5⅜ × 8½. 22487-2 Pa. $6.95

DRAWING THE LIVING FIGURE, Joseph Sheppard. Innovative approach to artistic anatomy focuses on specifics of surface anatomy, rather than muscles and bones. Over 170 drawings of live models in front, back and side views, and in widely varying poses. Accompanying diagrams. 177 illustrations. Introduction. Index. 144pp. 8⅜ × 11¼. 26723-7 Pa. $8.95

GOTHIC AND OLD ENGLISH ALPHABETS: 100 Complete Fonts, Dan X. Solo. Add power, elegance to posters, signs, other graphics with 100 stunning copyright-free alphabets: Blackstone, Dolbey, Germania, 97 more—including many lower-case, numerals, punctuation marks. 104pp. 8⅛ × 11. 24695-7 Pa. $8.95

HOW TO DO BEADWORK, Mary White. Fundamental book on craft from simple projects to five-bead chains and woven works. 106 illustrations. 142pp. 5⅜ × 8. 20697-1 Pa. $4.95

THE BOOK OF WOOD CARVING, Charles Marshall Sayers. Finest book for beginners discusses fundamentals and offers 34 designs. "Absolutely first rate . . . well thought out and well executed."—E. J. Tangerman. 118pp. 7¾ × 10⅝. 23654-4 Pa. $5.95

ILLUSTRATED CATALOG OF CIVIL WAR MILITARY GOODS: Union Army Weapons, Insignia, Uniform Accessories, and Other Equipment, Schuyler, Hartley, and Graham. Rare, profusely illustrated 1846 catalog includes Union Army uniform and dress regulations, arms and ammunition, coats, insignia, flags, swords, rifles, etc. 226 illustrations. 160pp. 9 × 12. 24939-5 Pa. $10.95

WOMEN'S FASHIONS OF THE EARLY 1900s: An Unabridged Republication of "New York Fashions, 1909," National Cloak & Suit Co. Rare catalog of mail-order fashions documents women's and children's clothing styles shortly after the turn of the century. Captions offer full descriptions, prices. Invaluable resource for fashion, costume historians. Approximately 725 illustrations. 128pp. 8⅜ × 11¼. 27276-1 Pa. $11.95

THE 1912 AND 1915 GUSTAV STICKLEY FURNITURE CATALOGS, Gustav Stickley. With over 200 detailed illustrations and descriptions, these two catalogs are essential reading and reference materials and identification guides for Stickley furniture. Captions cite materials, dimensions and prices. 112pp. 6½ × 9¼. 26676-1 Pa. $9.95

EARLY AMERICAN LOCOMOTIVES, John H. White, Jr. Finest locomotive engravings from early 19th century: historical (1804–74), main-line (after 1870), special, foreign, etc. 147 plates. 142pp. 11⅜ × 8¼. 22772-3 Pa. $10.95

THE TALL SHIPS OF TODAY IN PHOTOGRAPHS, Frank O. Braynard. Lavishly illustrated tribute to nearly 100 majestic contemporary sailing vessels: Amerigo Vespucci, Clearwater, Constitution, Eagle, Mayflower, Sea Cloud, Victory, many more. Authoritative captions provide statistics, background on each ship. 190 black-and-white photographs and illustrations. Introduction. 128pp. 8⅞ × 11¾. 27163-3 Pa. $13.95

EARLY NINETEENTH-CENTURY CRAFTS AND TRADES, Peter Stockham (ed.). Extremely rare 1807 volume describes to youngsters the crafts and trades of the day: brickmaker, weaver, dressmaker, bookbinder, ropemaker, saddler, many more. Quaint prose, charming illustrations for each craft. 20 black-and-white line illustrations. 192pp. 4⅝ × 6. 27293-1 Pa. $4.95

VICTORIAN FASHIONS AND COSTUMES FROM HARPER'S BAZAR, 1867–1898, Stella Blum (ed.). Day costumes, evening wear, sports clothes, shoes, hats, other accessories in over 1,000 detailed engravings. 320pp. 9⅜ × 12¼.
22990-4 Pa. $13.95

GUSTAV STICKLEY, THE CRAFTSMAN, Mary Ann Smith. Superb study surveys broad scope of Stickley's achievement, especially in architecture. Design philosophy, rise and fall of the Craftsman empire, descriptions and floor plans for many Craftsman houses, more. 86 black-and-white halftones. 31 line illustrations. Introduction. 208pp. 6½ × 9¼. 27210-9 Pa. $9.95

THE LONG ISLAND RAIL ROAD IN EARLY PHOTOGRAPHS, Ron Ziel. Over 220 rare photos, informative text document origin (1844) and development of rail service on Long Island. Vintage views of early trains, locomotives, stations, passengers, crews, much more. Captions. 8⅞ × 11¾. 26301-0 Pa. $13.95

THE BOOK OF OLD SHIPS: From Egyptian Galleys to Clipper Ships, Henry B. Culver. Superb, authoritative history of sailing vessels, with 80 magnificent line illustrations. Galley, bark, caravel, longship, whaler, many more. Detailed, informative text on each vessel by noted naval historian. Introduction. 256pp. 5⅜ × 8½. 27332-6 Pa. $6.95

TEN BOOKS ON ARCHITECTURE, Vitruvius. The most important book ever written on architecture. Early Roman aesthetics, technology, classical orders, site selection, all other aspects. Morgan translation. 331pp. 5⅜ × 8½. 20645-9 Pa. $8.95

THE HUMAN FIGURE IN MOTION, Eadweard Muybridge. More than 4,500 stopped-action photos, in action series, showing undraped men, women, children jumping, lying down, throwing, sitting, wrestling, carrying, etc. 390pp. 7⅞ × 10⅝.
20204-6 Clothbd. $24.95

TREES OF THE EASTERN AND CENTRAL UNITED STATES AND CANADA, William M. Harlow. Best one-volume guide to 140 trees. Full descriptions, woodlore, range, etc. Over 600 illustrations. Handy size. 288pp. 4½ × 6⅜.
20395-6 Pa. $5.95

SONGS OF WESTERN BIRDS, Dr. Donald J. Borror. Complete song and call repertoire of 60 western species, including flycatchers, juncoes, cactus wrens, many more—includes fully illustrated booklet. Cassette and manual 99913-0 $8.95

GROWING AND USING HERBS AND SPICES, Milo Miloradovich. Versatile handbook provides all the information needed for cultivation and use of all the herbs and spices available in North America. 4 illustrations. Index. Glossary. 236pp. 5⅜ × 8½. 25058-X Pa. $6.95

BIG BOOK OF MAZES AND LABYRINTHS, Walter Shepherd. 50 mazes and labyrinths in all—classical, solid, ripple, and more—in one great volume. Perfect inexpensive puzzler for clever youngsters. Full solutions. 112pp. 8⅛ × 11.
22951-3 Pa. $4.95

PIANO TUNING, J. Cree Fischer. Clearest, best book for beginner, amateur. Simple repairs, raising dropped notes, tuning by easy method of flattened fifths. No previous skills needed. 4 illustrations. 201pp. 5⅜ × 8½. 23267-0 Pa. $5.95

A SOURCE BOOK IN THEATRICAL HISTORY, A. M. Nagler. Contemporary observers on acting, directing, make-up, costuming, stage props, machinery, scene design, from Ancient Greece to Chekhov. 611pp. 5⅜ × 8½. 20515-0 Pa. $11.95

THE COMPLETE NONSENSE OF EDWARD LEAR, Edward Lear. All nonsense limericks, zany alphabets, Owl and Pussycat, songs, nonsense botany, etc., illustrated by Lear. Total of 320pp. 5⅜ × 8½. (USO) 20167-8 Pa. $6.95

VICTORIAN PARLOUR POETRY: An Annotated Anthology, Michael R. Turner. 117 gems by Longfellow, Tennyson, Browning, many lesser-known poets. "The Village Blacksmith," "Curfew Must Not Ring Tonight," "Only a Baby Small," dozens more, often difficult to find elsewhere. Index of poets, titles, first lines. xxiii + 325pp. 5⅜ × 8¼. 27044-0 Pa. $8.95

DUBLINERS, James Joyce. Fifteen stories offer vivid, tightly focused observations of the lives of Dublin's poorer classes. At least one, "The Dead," is considered a masterpiece. Reprinted complete and unabridged from standard edition. 160pp. 5³⁄₁₆ × 8¼. 26870-5 Pa. $1.00

THE HAUNTED MONASTERY and THE CHINESE MAZE MURDERS, Robert van Gulik. Two full novels by van Gulik, set in 7th-century China, continue adventures of Judge Dee and his companions. An evil Taoist monastery, seemingly supernatural events; overgrown topiary maze hides strange crimes. 27 illustrations. 328pp. 5⅜ × 8½. 23502-5 Pa. $7.95

THE BOOK OF THE SACRED MAGIC OF ABRAMELIN THE MAGE, translated by S. MacGregor Mathers. Medieval manuscript of ceremonial magic. Basic document in Aleister Crowley, Golden Dawn groups. 268pp. 5⅜ × 8½. 23211-5 Pa. $8.95

NEW RUSSIAN-ENGLISH AND ENGLISH-RUSSIAN DICTIONARY, M. A. O'Brien. This is a remarkably handy Russian dictionary, containing a surprising amount of information, including over 70,000 entries. 366pp. 4½ × 6⅛. 20208-9 Pa. $9.95

HISTORIC HOMES OF THE AMERICAN PRESIDENTS, Second, Revised Edition, Irvin Haas. A traveler's guide to American Presidential homes, most open to the public, depicting and describing homes occupied by every American President from George Washington to George Bush. With visiting hours, admission charges, travel routes. 175 photographs. Index. 160pp. 8¼ × 11. 26751-2 Pa. $10.95

NEW YORK IN THE FORTIES, Andreas Feininger. 162 brilliant photographs by the well-known photographer, formerly with *Life* magazine. Commuters, shoppers, Times Square at night, much else from city at its peak. Captions by John von Hartz. 181pp. 9¼ × 10¾. 23585-8 Pa. $12.95

INDIAN SIGN LANGUAGE, William Tomkins. Over 525 signs developed by Sioux and other tribes. Written instructions and diagrams. Also 290 pictographs. 111pp. 6⅛ × 9¼. 22029-X Pa. $3.50

ANATOMY: A Complete Guide for Artists, Joseph Sheppard. A master of figure drawing shows artists how to render human anatomy convincingly. Over 460 illustrations. 224pp. 8⅜ × 11¼. 27279-6 Pa. $10.95

MEDIEVAL CALLIGRAPHY: Its History and Technique, Marc Drogin. Spirited history, comprehensive instruction manual covers 13 styles (ca. 4th century thru 15th). Excellent photographs; directions for duplicating medieval techniques with modern tools. 224pp. 8⅜ × 11¼. 26142-5 Pa. $11.95

DRIED FLOWERS: How to Prepare Them, Sarah Whitlock and Martha Rankin. Complete instructions on how to use silica gel, meal and borax, perlite aggregate, sand and borax, glycerine and water to create attractive permanent flower arrangements. 12 illustrations. 32pp. 5⅜ × 8½. 21802-3 Pa. $1.00

EASY-TO-MAKE BIRD FEEDERS FOR WOODWORKERS, Scott D. Campbell. Detailed, simple-to-use guide for designing, constructing, caring for and using feeders. Text, illustrations for 12 classic and contemporary designs. 96pp. 5⅜ × 8½. 25847-5 Pa. $2.95

OLD-TIME CRAFTS AND TRADES, Peter Stockham. An 1807 book created to teach children about crafts and trades open to them as future careers. It describes in detailed, nontechnical terms 24 different occupations, among them coachmaker, gardener, hairdresser, lacemaker, shoemaker, wheelwright, copper-plate printer, milliner, trunkmaker, merchant and brewer. Finely detailed engravings illustrate each occupation. 192pp. 4⅝ × 6. 27398-9 Pa. $4.95

THE HISTORY OF UNDERCLOTHES, C. Willett Cunnington and Phyllis Cunnington. Fascinating, well-documented survey covering six centuries of English undergarments, enhanced with over 100 illustrations: 12th-century laced-up bodice, footed long drawers (1795), 19th-century bustles, 19th-century corsets for men, Victorian "bust improvers," much more. 272pp. 5⅜ × 8¼. 27124-2 Pa. $9.95

ARTS AND CRAFTS FURNITURE: The Complete Brooks Catalog of 1912, Brooks Manufacturing Co. Photos and detailed descriptions of more than 150 now very collectible furniture designs from the Arts and Crafts movement depict davenports, settees, buffets, desks, tables, chairs, bedsteads, dressers and more, all built of solid, quarter-sawed oak. Invaluable for students and enthusiasts of antiques, Americana and the decorative arts. 80pp. 6½ × 9¼. 27471-3 Pa. $7.95

HOW WE INVENTED THE AIRPLANE: An Illustrated History, Orville Wright. Fascinating firsthand account covers early experiments, construction of planes and motors, first flights, much more. Introduction and commentary by Fred C. Kelly. 76 photographs. 96pp. 8¼ × 11. 25662-6 Pa. $8.95

THE ARTS OF THE SAILOR: Knotting, Splicing and Ropework, Hervey Garrett Smith. Indispensable shipboard reference covers tools, basic knots and useful hitches; handsewing and canvas work, more. Over 100 illustrations. Delightful reading for sea lovers. 256pp. 5⅜ × 8½. 26440-8 Pa. $7.95

FRANK LLOYD WRIGHT'S FALLINGWATER: The House and Its History, Second, Revised Edition, Donald Hoffmann. A total revision—both in text and illustrations—of the standard document on Fallingwater, the boldest, most personal architectural statement of Wright's mature years, updated with valuable new material from the recently opened Frank Lloyd Wright Archives. "Fascinating"—*The New York Times*. 116 illustrations. 128pp. 9¼ × 10¾. 27430-6 Pa. $10.95

PHOTOGRAPHIC SKETCHBOOK OF THE CIVIL WAR, Alexander Gardner. 100 photos taken on field during the Civil War. Famous shots of Manassas, Harper's Ferry, Lincoln, Richmond, slave pens, etc. 244pp. 10⅝ × 8¼.
22731-6 Pa. $9.95

FIVE ACRES AND INDEPENDENCE, Maurice G. Kains. Great back-to-the-land classic explains basics of self-sufficient farming. The one book to get. 95 illustrations. 397pp. 5⅜ × 8½.
20974-1 Pa. $7.95

SONGS OF EASTERN BIRDS, Dr. Donald J. Borror. Songs and calls of 60 species most common to eastern U.S.: warblers, woodpeckers, flycatchers, thrushes, larks, many more in high-quality recording.
Cassette and manual 99912-2 $8.95

A MODERN HERBAL, Margaret Grieve. Much the fullest, most exact, most useful compilation of herbal material. Gigantic alphabetical encyclopedia, from aconite to zedoary, gives botanical information, medical properties, folklore, economic uses, much else. Indispensable to serious reader. 161 illustrations. 888pp. 6½ × 9¼. 2-vol. set. (USO)
Vol. I: 22798-7 Pa. $9.95
Vol. II: 22799-5 Pa. $9.95

HIDDEN TREASURE MAZE BOOK, Dave Phillips. Solve 34 challenging mazes accompanied by heroic tales of adventure. Evil dragons, people-eating plants, bloodthirsty giants, many more dangerous adversaries lurk at every twist and turn. 34 mazes, stories, solutions. 48pp. 8¼ × 11.
24566-7 Pa. $2.95

LETTERS OF W. A. MOZART, Wolfgang A. Mozart. Remarkable letters show bawdy wit, humor, imagination, musical insights, contemporary musical world; includes some letters from Leopold Mozart. 276pp. 5⅜ × 8½.
22859-2 Pa. $7.95

BASIC PRINCIPLES OF CLASSICAL BALLET, Agrippina Vaganova. Great Russian theoretician, teacher explains methods for teaching classical ballet. 118 illustrations. 175pp. 5⅜ × 8½.
22036-2 Pa. $4.95

THE JUMPING FROG, Mark Twain. Revenge edition. The original story of The Celebrated Jumping Frog of Calaveras County, a hapless French translation, and Twain's hilarious "retranslation" from the French. 12 illustrations. 66pp. 5⅜ × 8½.
22686-7 Pa. $3.95

BEST REMEMBERED POEMS, Martin Gardner (ed.). The 126 poems in this superb collection of 19th- and 20th-century British and American verse range from Shelley's "To a Skylark" to the impassioned "Renascence" of Edna St. Vincent Millay and to Edward Lear's whimsical "The Owl and the Pussycat." 224pp. 5⅜ × 8½.
27165-X Pa. $4.95

COMPLETE SONNETS, William Shakespeare. Over 150 exquisite poems deal with love, friendship, the tyranny of time, beauty's evanescence, death and other themes in language of remarkable power, precision and beauty. Glossary of archaic terms. 80pp. 5³⁄₁₆ × 8¼.
26686-9 Pa. $1.00

BODIES IN A BOOKSHOP, R. T. Campbell. Challenging mystery of blackmail and murder with ingenious plot and superbly drawn characters. In the best tradition of British suspense fiction. 192pp. 5⅜ × 8½.
24720-1 Pa. $5.95

THE INFLUENCE OF SEA POWER UPON HISTORY, 1660–1783, A. T. Mahan. Influential classic of naval history and tactics still used as text in war colleges. First paperback edition. 4 maps. 24 battle plans. 640pp. 5⅜ × 8½.
25509-3 Pa. $12.95

THE STORY OF THE TITANIC AS TOLD BY ITS SURVIVORS, Jack Winocour (ed.). What it was really like. Panic, despair, shocking inefficiency, and a little heroism. More thrilling than any fictional account. 26 illustrations. 320pp. 5⅜ × 8½.
20610-6 Pa. $8.95

FAIRY AND FOLK TALES OF THE IRISH PEASANTRY, William Butler Yeats (ed.). Treasury of 64 tales from the twilight world of Celtic myth and legend: "The Soul Cages," "The Kildare Pooka," "King O'Toole and his Goose," many more. Introduction and Notes by W. B. Yeats. 352pp. 5⅜ × 8½.
26941-8 Pa. $8.95

BUDDHIST MAHAYANA TEXTS, E. B. Cowell and Others (eds.). Superb, accurate translations of basic documents in Mahayana Buddhism, highly important in history of religions. The Buddha-karita of Asvaghosha, Larger Sukhavativyuha, more. 448pp. 5⅜ × 8½.
25552-2 Pa. $9.95

ONE TWO THREE . . . INFINITY: Facts and Speculations of Science, George Gamow. Great physicist's fascinating, readable overview of contemporary science: number theory, relativity, fourth dimension, entropy, genes, atomic structure, much more. 128 illustrations. Index. 352pp. 5⅜ × 8½.
25664-2 Pa. $8.95

ENGINEERING IN HISTORY, Richard Shelton Kirby, et al. Broad, nontechnical survey of history's major technological advances: birth of Greek science, industrial revolution, electricity and applied science, 20th-century automation, much more. 181 illustrations. ". . . excellent . . ."—Isis. Bibliography. vii + 530pp. 5⅜ × 8¼.
26412-2 Pa. $14.95

Prices subject to change without notice.

Available at your book dealer or write for free catalog to Dept. GI, Dover Publications, Inc., 31 East 2nd St., Mineola, N.Y. 11501. Dover publishes more than 500 books each year on science, elementary and advanced mathematics, biology, music, art, literary history, social sciences and other areas.